Principles for Dynamic Leadership

Back to Basics

Dr. Kobin Archary, Ph.D.

Principles for Dynamic Leadership

Back to Basics

Dr. Kobin Archary, Ph.D.

ISBN 978-1-61529-152-6

Copyright © 2014 Kobin Archary

Vision Publishing
1672 Main Street E 109
Ramona, CA 92065
1 800-9-VISION
www.booksbyvision.com

All rights reserved worldwide. No part of this book may be reproduced in any manner without the written permission of the author except in brief quotations embodied in critical articles or reviews.

Acknowledgements

I would like to place on record my sincere thanks and appreciation to my Lord Jesus Christ. This was a difficult task brought to completion, primarily due to His continual impartation of wisdom and strength.

To my wife Radha, children Nigel Wayne and Rochelle Ann– your inspiration and expectation of me to succeed has always been a driving force.

To Dr. Robert Munien and Pastor Judy Munien – thank you for your mentorship and guidance.

To Pastor Stanley Kitty, sincere thanks and appreciation for setting foundational principles and disciplines during the early years of ministry.

To those who have taken the time to read this script, your constructive feedback has been highly valued.

To all my family and friends who have provided unwavering support -- thank you.

Finally to my Angel – Chrysander Anastasia – who went to be with the Lord on 3 May 2001 at the age of 6. To you my baby, I dedicate this book.

Chrysander Anastasia

Born: 7 February 1995

With Christ: 3 May 2001

Age: 6 years

Table of Contents

Acknowledgements 3

Forewords 7

Preface...11

Chapter 1 Understanding Leadership 13

Chapter 2 Leadership Defined 23

Chapter 3 Qualities of Leadership 33

Chapter 4 Know Thyself...53

Chapter 5 Theories of Motivation 57

Chapter 6 Communication..67

Chapter 7 Paradigm Shift..75

Chapter 8 The Challenge of Change 83

Chapter 9 Stress Management 95

Chapter 10 Powerbased Leadership 113

Chapter 11 Technology of a Leader 135

Conclusion 183

Leadership Dynamics...187

Bibliography 199

Forewords

It is a profound honor to have been asked by Dr. Kobin Archary to write a foreword to Principles for Dynamic Leadership. I have had the privilege of watching Kobin work in the corporate world and also bring his practical knowledge to the Church environment. He resigned from the corporate world and went on to start his very successful business and dedicate most of his time in the Church as a servant leader. Dr. Kobin also serves as the Southern African Director of Vision International Education Network.

The dictionary defines authority in terms of command, control, power, sway, rule, supremacy, domination, dominion, strength, might. But its antonyms are civility, servitude, weakness, and follower. Moral influence is gained by following the principles. Moral dominion is achieved through servitude, contribution, service, where the greatest becomes the servant of all through sacrifice.

"Leaders hold their positions purely because they are able to appeal to conscience and to reason with those who support them and bosses hold their positions because they appeal to fear of punishment and hope of reward. Leaders work in the open, and bosses in covert. Leaders lead and bosses drive" – Theodore Roosevelt.

Dr. Kobin's clear call is for a new paradigm shift from managers who drive people to achieve goals to the concept of stewardship and redefine leadership as a servant.

Matthew 20:25-27

But Jesus called them to Himself and said, "You know that the rulers of the Gentiles lord it over them, and those who are great exercise authority over them. Yet it shall not be so among you; but whoever desires to become great among you, let him be your servant. And whoever desires to be first among you, let him be your slave." (NKJV)

I recommend this book to all those who are called to be leaders.

Dr. Robert Munien
Grace Outreach Ministries

Each generation needs to discover and train new leaders, not only to meet current needs but also to prepare for future challenges and changes. This book seeks to present a practical theology of leadership based on the principles taught and illustrated in the Bible.

Leaders are people – God's people – God's chosen people – chosen to do His will and His work and to help others to do His work. Dr. Kobin Archary is one such leader used in our local church, Grace Outreach Ministries, in Durban, South Africa as well as globally, who is functionally competent as a dynamic 21st century leader.

This book is designed to equip and bring the church to a place of operational competence in its understanding of leadership. True leaders never ask others to do what they themselves are unwilling to do. Dr. Kobin is a true leader, and therefore, I highly recommend him and his book.

Pastor Judy Munien MBA

There remains an age old controversy regarding leaders, are leaders born or are they made? From my experience, the answer is yes, no, and maybe. Yes, in certain circumstances, a crisis or a void can suddenly thrust someone into a leadership role by default. Yet, those leaders birthed by crisis are usually temporary, they return to their more mundane callings after the crisis is gone. Many leaders, especially those who are university trained, start well, but they often fade when the going gets tough. Great and lasting leaders seem to have certain intrinsic qualities, such as tenacity, vision, a sense of honor, duty, and compassion. One could add to that, through the crucible of life experience: knowledge, understanding, and wisdom.

In addition, having an ability to cast vision and persuade in a specific direction, along with the ability to motivate someone to action. These qualities seem to be both intrinsic and external (learned). Such are the dynamics of leadership.

In this excellent work by my friend, colleague, former student, business leader and church administrator, Dr. Kobin provides many excellent insights. These insights are the qualities, attitudes, and skills necessary to become a healthy and successful leader. Without a doubt, healthy leaders are needed in the marketplace and the church. Dr. Archary, with precision and care, presents the keys to becoming a healthy leader and sustaining that leadership for the long haul.

Though the entire work is excellent, I was most impressed with his chapter on paradigm shift. It is a challenge to change, grow, and become all that God has created us to be as leaders. It is the challenge of every growing mature leader.

This work will become a part of our curriculum at Vision International University; it is a great addition that will strengthen present and future leaders for generations to come.

Stan E. DeKoven, Ph.D.
President
Vision International University

Preface

One of the fundamental principles that many organizations are discovering is that the success of their existence, sustenance and growth largely depends on leadership at the helm. Leadership is fast becoming a driving force that will take an organization to the next level. Non performing companies or organizations are primarily over managed and under led. Hence, most successful companies have migrated from the traditional management model to leadership principle adoption. After reading this book, you will have a clearer view of how important this shift in paradigm is.

This is no different from the church today. There are clear indications, often evidenced, that there exists a need for leaders, to be functionally competent according to biblical norms and standards. If leaders do not model the required behavior, those that follow will disengage, especially when there is a lack of correlation with the leader's action versus their code of conduct and value system. This has been a serious concern, resulting in pursuing research on this topic with vigor and determination.

The research has taken approximately four years to complete, basically a combination of my experience, both secular and church. This research is also based on models that I am convinced, if followed, would positively impact our organizations and churches.

Also, included is research based on scientific management, using several theories and behavioral models by prominent psychologists. The reason for this is that rarely are there any considerations given to key components that constitute the psychological profile of people. Ultimately, leadership is about people. We need to understand the reasons we exist, and the key drivers that motivate us on a day to day basis. We are emotional beings, sometimes complex and varying, depending on the circumstances and situations we face at any given time. To understand people is to lead effectively. Alternately, to lead effectively is to understand people.

The research has been intense, consisting of in the region of fifty-one books. Some of the books written by prolific authors on leadership have been researched. The challenge was to extract synergies from these different and diverse writings, together with my ultimate objective and create a working document that covers important facets of leadership. In the final analysis, the leadership examples in the Bible, particularly that which was modelled by Jesus, while on the face of the earth, forms the foundation on which leadership principles should be built upon.

Even though, biblically based, the leadership principles are the same, irrespective of its application to secular organizations, church work, or for that matter, personal adoption of principles.

Chapter 1

Understanding Leadership

Introduction

More and more every day, there seems to be a shift from what we traditionally know as management, to a more influential and vibrant model called leadership. Leadership is a phenomenon that has existed since the beginning of time, but for some unknown reason, is not as dominant as management practices in today's world. Great accomplishments in history have been recorded through leadership. We are dependent on leaders in every field, whether it is in medicine, education, government, commerce, etc. Obviously, there are leaders who have had a positive impact, and then there are those who are remembered for their atrocities. By classification, both types are leaders. However, leaders, by and large, we refer to, are those who exude positive influences and connotations. Hence, whenever we talk about or discuss leaders, we are referring to people who have had a positive impact on organizations, and especially, lives of people.

Society places a high premium on individuals who are in positions of leadership and more emphatic are the responsibilities of leadership. However, a challenge that the world faces today in every facet, is the shortage of equipped, trained and influential leaders.

Just about everyone has inherent leadership traits that can be harnessed and nurtured. They may possess certain skills, but lack training and development, which necessitate them to function as competent leaders. The dilemma, or challenge, is the lack of formal training or mentorship programs, which provide training and development needs within an organization that will help facilitate knowledge, in order to enhance leadership development. Leadership can be nerve-racking and exhausting. Every new day poses new challenges. We are living in a world of dynamic changing cultural trends. In today's pluralistic world, cultural lines run across whole societies. Old solutions may not, necessarily be the answer to current problems. Past achievements may turn out to be liabilities. This is happening on a global scale, particularly in developing nations. Hence, the ability to function with some level of accuracy and competence is a necessary requirement for leadership in today's dynamic environment.

In many of our organizations, situations arise as a result of desperation to fill leadership positions. In order to move forward, for whatever reason, available people whom we think have some potential or are thought to be capable of functioning as a leader, are given this responsibility. This person strives to function, sometimes under duress, to the best of their ability. It then becomes acceptable, after a short period of time, that recognition is given together with the responsibilities, that this person is a sanctioned leader within the organization. Most times this exercise becomes a cloning process based on previous successes of other people. These leaders are likely to develop a culture specific vision that is simply a projection of others previous achievement. This is similarly to what Shakespeare referred to when he said "some are born great, some achieve greatness and some have greatness thrust upon them." In leadership – some are born leaders and some have leadership thrust upon them. However, it must be understood that learned behavior is also an important ingredient in leadership development.

This could be a situation where we have, an enthusiastic and willing person, yet untrained and under developed, trying to function as a leader. Invariably, they find themselves in position of responsibility without authority. They are indecisive, constantly making and retracting decisions. Their inability to operate efficiently will always cast doubt or blame on the system or others, for inadequate help or authority delegated to them. Lack of clear articulation of expected outcomes, from leaders who fail to be role models will result in negative consequences, both in the short and long term. This will, most likely, precipitate a crisis, for both the organization and the leader or leadership unless there is a self-correct mechanism to keep leadership continuously vibrant. Ultimately, it has been proven, people stay with leaders more than they do with organizations. We have failed to read and accurately interpret the signs of the times. This will create chaos in relational harmonies that binds organizations together.

People are also given the responsibility of leadership, because current leadership is convinced, based on their perception, knowledge and understanding, however limited that may be, that certain people are suited for leadership positions.

There could be one of many reasons.

- We may like them – admitted or not, some people have favorites.
- They are faithful members, workers, employees etc.
- They have financial backing.
- They maybe influential or have influential connections.
- Nepotism – this seems to be a big player.

The list can go on.

These types of leadership appointees, in most cases, become strong defenders of the status quo. They become stringent advocates of a type of conservatism. They will always have a deep seated aversion to risk taking and their innovation is reinforced as a result of their training, development and education inculcated in them by their appointer. Sadly, they eventually become the reflection of the people they were appointed by. While their organization ages and dwindles in numbers, they will always maintain a non-conforming, irrelevant, and redundant mind-set that will eventually lead to their demise.

On the other hand, some people find an attraction of a safe haven from the pressures of the secular world. Full time pastoral ministry becomes an ideal choice of employment and income generation. Generally, these people are also less likely to be risk takers and are, therefore, less prepared to pay a price of sacrifice. These people feel safe in an environment of conservatism and security of a traditional culture. While everything in life changes, they will always remain in a familiar place, an anchor away from the fast-paced world.

Eddie Gibbs, author of *Leadership Next,* quotes Steve Nicholson on "How to Recruit a Church Planting Team" which inadvertently, is leadership.

He strongly advises that decisions should be made on the basis of the functions that individuals on the team will fulfill. If they happen to be friends, or become friends in the process is a bonus. He is concerned that working on the basis of friendship may mean that better qualified people are excluded and that friends may be retained in positions where they are ineffective to avoid damaging the friendship.[1]

This will ultimately create a chain reaction. Appointing untrained and underdeveloped leaders will have repercussions with far reaching negative consequences. There are, in many cases, concerns about current leadership capabilities, who appoint these untrained leaders based on understandings and perceptions that are inaccurate.

This has proven to be one of the greatest weaknesses in any organization. This, sooner or later, creates problems that could take years and sometimes, generations to rectify, most times at great cost and reputation to the organization. How often have we tried to put out fires, fix, manage by crisis and ultimately do damage control because of untrained and under developed leader's decisions and actions? In cases of liability, the person in charge is held responsible, because of mishaps, statements, and bad or improper decisions taken by leaders under their jurisdiction.

Perceptions are formed of organizations that create huge problems with lasting implications. This task becomes difficult, and to undo an unfavorable situation will sometimes require exceptional skills. This

---

[1] Gibbs Eddie – Leadership Next – Intervarsity Press – UK - 2005

is time consuming and costly, never mind the infringement or risk on the reputation of the organization.

Currently, it is very possible that we are also dealing with different mindsets. Leadership of the "old school" is very much alive and prevalent in many organizations that exist today. Sometimes, old mindsets and habits have to change in order to set a new and innovative direction. The great weakness in many of these organizations is the inability to change or to keep abreast with currently dynamic changing trends. They have not built infrastructure to deal with constant and relevant changes. Unless there is a transition to healthier models, churches and organizations will disintegrate or fossilize as a result of constant conflict. This is one of the numerous reasons why so many churches and organizations have lost, and are continually losing members or employees.

They are continuously disseminating the same level of information with no noticeable change or growth. Often times, you will find that the leadership mentality reflected in the head leader is transferred to leadership down the ranks. This becomes the yard-stick of measurement in some cases, with detrimental effects. Most often, churches and organizations become personality driven. The culture of the organization is engineered by the leadership and is then embraced by the followers or members. This culture is contagious and can be infectious to the detriment of the church or organization.

Note the word "challenge" used in the second paragraph. To ensure that we have trained leaders functioning within our organizations is indeed a challenge. The challenge here is to ensure that, before anyone is appointed as a leader, they are trained with the necessary skills to function in that particular capacity, depending on what the actual functions of their portfolio entails. This is the basic foundation of leadership skills development. The rest is left to experience and more important, the leader continues to study, according to their individual needs. There is no "I have arrived" situation because training and development is an ongoing continuous and dynamic process. Great leaders are great learners. Learning assumes an attitude of submission. If you are not teachable, you are not approachable.

Here are some excellent expositions from the book of Proverbs:

- Let the wise listen and add to their learning, and let the discerning get guidance. Proverbs 1:5
- The way of the fool seems right to him, but a wise man listens to advice. Proverbs 12:15
- Plans fail for lack of counsel, but with many advisors they succeed. Proverbs 15:22
- Listen to advice and accept instruction, and in the end you will be wise. Proverbs 19:20

The secular world, which operates on the Babylonian system, adopts this strategy and has proven to produce success. The Babylonian system rarely ever appoints untrained persons in positions of leadership or responsibility, because of the harm this appointment will bring to the organization. Leadership skills are generally identified, training and skills development is executed and only then are potential leaders placed in positions of leadership. If such attention and professionalism is adopted by this system, why then, have we failed to accord the same level of, if not more, importance within our church organizations?

Leadership should identify key candidates, and then train them to assume positions of leadership. Cyril Barber, in his book *Effective Leadership* quotes George Olmstead, retired General of the Unites States Army, writing in *The Industrial Banker*, pointed out that "if our free enterprise system is to prove its superiority…our greatest hope lies in finding and developing young men and women with talents for leadership. Private enterprise can only be as strong as the men and women who run our business. Our future survival depends upon the success of our programs of leadership development – not only in business but all areas of our national life. This then must be our objective. Our program for leadership development must succeed."[2]

We have failed to implement processes to ensure that we have a system in place, to ensure that necessary training and development is implemented to assist potential leaders within our organizations. Little or no attention is given to this.

The following may be some of the reasons:

- Do not have the know-how, or lack of expertise in training and development.
- Do not budget for or to invest in training and development
- Lack of time – failure to plan adequately
- Refuse to accept change or new strategies
- Financial – generally, anything that costs money is continuously procrastinated or often given little or no attention

Again, the list can go on. There are no quick fixes.

We are merely managing organizations instead of leading. Hence, we are consistently managing by crisis. We have witnessed the gradual weakening and decline of denominational structures that have existed for years. There is a new generation that is emerging, a generation with intelligence and insight.

We need to realize the serious responsibility we have been entrusted with and the repercussions of poor or failed leadership. We are dealing with people whose emotions, if mishandled or scarred, will suffer serious negative consequences. The sooner we accept this, the sooner we must accept the responsibility that goes with this.

---

[2] Barber Cyril-Effective Leadership – Cox and Wyman – Berkshire - 2004

Literally speaking, there are no excuses that can justify poor leadership in this day and time. The amount of resources available today, compared to previously, is insurmountable.

The successful organizations that exist today are because of great leaders!

George Halsey, in his book, *Supervising People* states:

"It has been demonstrated time and time again that almost any person of normal intelligence and sincere desire to be of service to people can acquire considerable skill in the art of supervising people, **if he will study its principles and methods and apply them thoughtfully, conscientiously, and persistently**".[3]

There are two glaring issues or challenges that have to be addressed: firstly, how can leaders, now in position be re-trained so that they understand changing trends both locally and globally?

Secondly, how do we identify a new generation of leaders, train and empower them, so that their level of confidence is developed to execute their duties with authority and confidence.

We need to prioritize identifying and resourcing leaders of a new generation mentality. This requires new thinking patterns and strategies. We need to sometimes break out of our old molds. This may be a radical approach, but it does not imply that there has to be a total eradication of old type leadership. There has to be a combining of insights and skills or lateral thinking. Leaders must become transformational influencers in these times of cultural transition.

Of vital importance, note the specific condition stipulated in the words of George Halsey as quoted.

---

[3] Halsey George – Supervising people, quoted by Killian, Ray in Managers Must Lead – New York -1966

Hence, Back to Basics

Chapter 2

Leadership Defined

Having worked in different levels of management up to the position of senior management, I have always been intrigued by the subject of leadership. One of the greatest challenges I have enjoyed over the past years, and one of the most difficult I might add, is this ability to lead or manage people. During my years as a manger, I have seen other managers fail because of their inability to adapt to changing environments and trends. Change is inevitable and, therefore, the ability to keep abreast is of vital importance. The greatest contributor to many of these failures is that there is a lack of change of mind-sets. People, generally, have the tendency to resist change. This is a natural phenomenon of inertia. People become set in their ways and therefore, any new ideas and changes that are introduced are generally seen as interference. This is very prevalent among the "loner types. "They often see themselves as the unquestionable head. It is a case of "you cannot teach an old dog new tricks." This is an insult, even to an old dog. Hence, leadership is about bringing people together for the purpose of creative synergy.[4]

Old leadership and management styles are not necessarily wrong or outdated. We cannot ignore old leadership and management styles that have been tried, tested and have produced positive results over the years. Even though some of these old traits have become terminal and must die, there must be a resurrection or new and innovative methods of leading. However, times have changed, people have changed. Therefore, it is necessary, while we have learned and adopted old leadership styles, we cannot ignore new and innovative leadership styles. The major challenge is not only the acquisition of

---

[4] Gibbs Eddie – Leadership Next- Intervarsity press – UK - 2005

new insights and skills, but also the unlearning and learning process that enables a leader to grow and develop on a continual basis.

Training needs to be developed and designed according to the needs of the organization and then micro managed to that of individuals. Interrelationship between theory, practice, gifting and callings must be evident. However, most times, training is time consuming and expensive resulting in a bottleneck rather than an available fountain source for future leaders. These bottlenecks have to be dealt with and opportunities made accessible for emerging leaders.

Currently, there is a shift in paradigms, a migration from management to leadership. Leadership has become an enabling force helping organizations and people to perform and develop, which implies that a sophisticated alignment is achieved – of people's needs and the aims of the organization.

Unlike management, leadership in the modern age requires attitudes and behaviors which characteristics and relates to humanity. The concept of serving forms the fundamental principle to the leadership role. Unlike management, that fosters personal status, authority, gains at the expense of others, leadership is the platform to serve. Management is about processes, leadership is mostly about behavior. Management relies on tangible measureable capabilities such as planning, the use of systems and processes etc. Leadership does engage these skills, but relies on less tangible and less measurable things like trust, inspiration, attitude, personal character etc. Most organizations are embracing these phenomena. It is proving to be the current day trend. Many universities are now offering more leadership qualifications as compared to previous management development programs.

In order to be relevant in today's environment, a great story to remember is the extinction of the dinosaurs. We risk a similar fate – unless we adapt to current and changing trends, we will become extinct.

Tom Peters and Robert Waterman Jr. authors of, *In Search of Excellence,* describe leadership as follows:

Leadership is many things. It is patient, usually boring coalition building. It is the purposeful seeding of cabals that one hopes will result in the appropriate ferment in the bowels of the organization. It is meticulous shifting the attention of the institution through the mundane language of management systems. It is altering agendas so that new priorities get enough attention. It is being visible when things are awry and invisible when things are going well. It is building a loyal team at the top that speaks more or less with one voice. It is listening carefully much of the time, frequently speaking with encouragement and reinforcing words with believable action. It is being tough when necessary, and it is the occasional naked use of power – or the "subtle accumulation of nuances, a hundred things done a little better", as Henry Kissinger once put it.[5]

I found this to be one of the most descriptive definitions, which basically sums up the entire concept of leadership defined. Even though, this sounds very much like a corporate definition, the fundamental basics of leadership are clearly evident.

Leadership and motivational abilities are very closely related, as strong leadership will motivate and motivation shows good leadership. Leadership can also be defined as *"**the ability to inspire willing action**"*[6]

Emphasis is placed on willing. One thing experience has proven over and over again, down through the ages, is that when any group of people are thrown together for any length of time or for any project, a leader will emerge from that group – one to whom the group will listen and give their confidence and support. A position on the organizational chart or title alone cannot make a person a genuine leader. A leader must have certain traits and skills or he will fail. It

---

[5] Peters Thomas and Robert Waterman, Jr. – In Search of Excellence – New York 1982
[6] Strafford John – Effective Management – Heinemann London - 1987

has been proven that skills can be learned and traits developed if a person is willing to exert an effort based on strong desire and hunger for success.

Generally, a leader, no matter how successful he has been, cannot actually develop another person. He encourages a person to develop him or herself from within. Thus, leadership, by and large, is self-initiated.

Once we understand and identify the methods and characteristics of an admired or seasoned leader, we can take steps to develop these skills and traits ourselves.

Leadership is also a calling. Some people have natural leadership gifts. With ease, they work well with others with great motivation and produce the desired results.

Romans12: 6-8 reads

"Having gifts that differ accordingly to the grace given to us, let us use them: if prophecy, in proportion to our faith; if service, in our serving; he who teaches, in his teaching; he who exhorts, in his exhortation; he who contributes, in liberality; he who gives aid, with zeal; he who does acts of mercy, with cheerfulness."

Unfortunately, not all people fall into these categories.

Psalms 78:72 gives a tribute to a good leader – **"with upright heart he tendered them and guided them with skillful hands"**.

Words like "management" may be twentieth century terms, yet the skills needed for effective managerial skills are as ancient as the Old Testament.[7]

Again, we need to be reminded on a continual basis that an important ingredient in leadership essentially involves service. In the secular

---

[7] D'Souza Anthony – Leadership – Paulines Publications - 2003

world the word service sounds out of place. Leadership in the world denotes power, authority, honor, prestige or personal advantage.

We also have the teachings of Jesus, still rated currently the most influential leader that ever walked the face of the earth. He himself epitomized this approach to leadership. He showed his disciples how to lead by his own examples of selfless service.[8] This will be discussed in detail under "Technology of a Leader."

John R Moth said –

> **I have in mind the use of the word leadership which our Lord doubtless had in mind when He said,**
>
> **"He who would be the greater among you shall be a servant of all." Leadership in the sense of rendering the maximum of service; leadership in the sense of the largest selflessness; leadership in the sense of unswerving and unceasing absorption in the greatest work of the world, the building up of the Kingdom of our Lord Jesus Christ.[9]**

Anthony D'Souza in his book Leadership sums up with the following:

- Seeks to be of service, rather than dominate.
- Encourages and inspires.
- Respects rather than exploits others' personalities.
- Reflects, prays, and acts on Jesus Christ's words, "whoever wishes to be first among you, shall be your servant, even as the Son of Man came not to be served, but to serve, and to give his life as a ransom for many" (Mt 20:27,28)[10]

---

[8] D'Souza Anthony-Developing the Leader within You-Singapore-1994

[9] Sanders J. Oswald – (Quoted by Sanders) - Spiritual Leadership – Moody Press - 1967

[10] D'Souza Anthony – Leadership – Paulines Publications - 2003

This defines leadership within a Christian context.

There are hundreds of definitions of leadership. Some of these are very complex. However, the simplest definition is that which was made by Dr. Hendricks – Professor from the Dallas Theological Seminary – "a leader is someone who leads." Don't be fooled by the simplicity of this definition.

We must not confuse leadership with status. Even in large corporations and government agencies, the top ranking person may simply be number 1. We have all occasionally encountered the top persons who could not lead a squad of seven year olds to the ice cream counter.[11]

Leaders come in many forms, with many styles and diverse qualifications. The fact is there are many kinds of leaders, and this has implications for leadership education. Most of those seeking to develop potential leaders have in mind one ideal model that is inevitably constricting. We should give people a sense of the many types of leaders and styles of leadership, and encourage them to move toward those models that are right for them.[12]

Robert Keating says:

Leadership is service, in the sense that it seeks to meet the needs of another or of the group by performing needed functions. Sometimes strong directive power is effective leadership, such as when a group has lost its sense of direction or purpose; with another group, or at another time when the group is functioning well in its relationships and has its directions clear, non-directive styles of leadership are needed. Sometimes the group needs to be encouraged and supported; at other times it may need to be reoriented. Effective leadership serves the needs of the group.[13]

---

[11] Gardner John – On Leadership – The Free Press - 1990

[12] Ibid

[13] Keating Charles L – The Leadership Book – New York – Paulist Press, 1982

Basically – Anthony D'Souza sums up by stating – two major parts of leadership are:[14]

- Task orientated
- Relationship orientated

It is important to distinguish between leading and managing. Managing is usually tied with some sort of organizational structure. Managing is also based on power structures and on the principle of rule with authority or a chain of command. The true leader may have no organizational structure at all. He simply leads. Among other things he is a visionary who has the ability and potential to see the big picture with the end result on the horizon.

Here is an inspiring story of a leader who brings a whole new meaning to visionary leadership and further validates the above.

In 1947, a professor at the University of Chicago, Dr. Chandrasekhar, was scheduled to teach a class in advanced astrophysics. The Professor was living in Wisconsin. He planned to commute to Chicago twice a week, even though the class was held during winter. He encountered the very worst weather the Midwest could throw at him.

The Professor had second thoughts about teaching the class as only two students had signed up for the course. He thought of the distance, time away from his family and he thought of the snow and the ice. But, then he thought of the two students. He decided to follow through on his commitment to teach. He had obviously hoped for more than two students, yet perhaps those two students would be worth the time investment.

Ten years later, Dr. Chandrasekhar was very pleased to hear that the two young men, Chen Ning Yang and Tsung-Dao Lee both were awarded the Nobel Prize in physics in 1957.

---

[14] D'Souza Anthony – Leadership – Paulines Publications - 2003

In 1983, Dr. Chandrasekhar was awarded the same order. You might say that the class was worth the effort. The Professor who demonstrated his leadership abilities in being willing to teach just two young motivated students obviously passed along some values and character as well as a syllabus.[15]

This is a classic definition of leadership against all odds. Many great men and women have emerged through sacrificial commitment of people like Professor Chandrasekhar.

There are many more examples that can be used to define leadership. In the final analysis, it has got to do with who you are, and how do you define yourself as a leader. A true definition of how you rate yourself ultimately comes from within you. But, remember, fruits of leadership are very evident. Leaders do not just see an opportunity; they are the first to seize an opportunity.

Leadership is about inclusion. There are no class distinctions, social segregations or class differentiated systems. In the emerging church there are no passive consumers, but inquisitive participators and innovative thinkers. Every person makes a contribution which is unique, in relation to the context of the entire organization. Leadership thrives on relationships. Hence, relationship building and maintenance of these relationships are of significant importance. Once these are damaged or destroyed, for whatever reason, and not fixed in time, will result in a liquidation process or the start of the demise of a ministry. Assumption of indispensability by any leader will produce results!

Leadership is centrally concerned with people. The leadership role is an inevitable reflection of people's needs and challenges in modern life. Leadership is, therefore, a profound concept with increasingly complex implications, driven by a fast changing world.

Finally, a point to always remember, in the world of leadership, we operate under the misguided assumption that because we are leaders,

---

[15] Farrar Steven – Standing Tall – Questar Publishers - 1994

we do not need to be led. This conclusion will ultimately lead to demise or stagnation of leaders.

Chapter 3

Qualities of Leadership

Authors James Kouzes and Barry Posner surveyed nearly 1500 managers from around the USA, sponsored by the American Management Association. They based their research on "what values, personal traits, or characteristics do you look for and admire in your superiors?"

More than 225 values, traits, and characteristics were identified. These were reduced to 15 categories, forming a core value list. Interestingly, the highlighted categories were integrity, truthful, trustworthy, character and convictions.[16]

In a subsequent study, after several executive seminars at different locations, more than 2600 top-level managers completed a checklist of superior leadership characteristics. These checklists ranked honesty ahead of competency, intelligence, and inspiring.

In another study conducted by the Columbia Graduate School of Business, surveying more than 1500 top executives in twenty countries, the study looked into strategies for growth, areas of expertise, and personal characteristics of an ideal CEO. Ethics was rated most highly. In summary, they wanted a leader to be beyond reproach.[17]

Modern researches in pursuance of establishing the key fundamentals of the composition of a leader, have established two key components or characteristics. One was being task specialists, and the other, social-emotional experts.

---

[16] Kouzes and Posner- The Leadership Challenge -
[17] Ibid

The task specialist was emotionally estranged from both individuals and the group. Their strength lies in their ability to organize, set goals and direct activities towards achieving objectives. They excel in organizational skills and at the same time maintaining emotional distance.

The social emotional expert, on the other hand, maintains group morale and harmony. He also has the ability to be a great problem solver. He has an emotional attachment with the group, particularly where functioning necessitates personal relationships.

However, not every leader has the ability to play both roles. Nehemiah was one of the few who had the ability to function in both these roles. This will be covered under "Technology of a Leader."

Let's look at God's criteria for selection:

Abraham and Sarah were a highly unlikely couple from Chaldea. Joseph the youngest of 12 brothers was scoffed at and made fun of by his older siblings. Moses was rejected by his own people. David was not taken seriously by his family. The twelve disciples that Jesus chose, mostly from the working class, were men with no formal education. None of them came with any religious expertise.

What became of them was the final conclusion of why they were originally chosen.

The definite set of specifics can vary, but can be very difficult to narrow down the exact qualities that can emphatically define, or conclude leadership holistically. Earlier studies of leadership tried to explain leadership by pointing out leaders' superior qualities of personality and character which separated them from their followers. Early in the century, Thomas Carlyle assumed the "great men theory" of leadership. He argued that world progress came about because of the individual achievements of great men.

This "great man" theory frequently recurs in literature. Writers usually pose it this way: "Do great men cause great times or do great times cause great men?" Shakespeare came down on both sides of the debate when he wrote that "some are born great, some achieve greatness, and some have greatness thrust upon them." To which Kelly added that others purchase it; some win it by strength, force, or nepotism; and a few marry into it.[18]

The renowned educator and counsellor, James J. Gill, in *Educating for Leadership* states that:

The essential qualities and skills involved in leadership can be learned and developed through education and experience. People can learn to communicate clearly, to make effective decisions, to motivate and inspire, to maintain and show respect for and trust subordinates, to be just in making judgments, to instruct clearly and to be patient with mistakes, to be loyal to followers and tough in their behalf, to be humble and open to new ideas and different opinions, to keep a sense of humor, and to know how to relax.[19]

During the decades prior to World War II, research on leadership assumed that we could explain a leader's skill by identifying psychological (and at times even physiological) traits that manifest themselves in superior abilities. Shortly after World War II, Ralph M. Stogdill published a benchmark study in which he reviewed 124 studies of psychological traits of leaders. He asked, "What psychological traits distinguished leaders from followers?"[20]

Stodgill argued that psychological traits by themselves have little predictive significance. In combinations, however, they show distinct leadership qualities.[21]

For the purposes of this exercise I have used the following, which should give us a general overview of what the requirements and qualities of leadership should be. These by no means, are the

---

[18] D'Souza Anthony – Leadership – Paulines Publications - 2003

[19] Gill James – Educating for Leadership – from Human Development – 1983 - Stogdill

[20] D'Souza Anthony – Leadership – Paulines Publications - 2003

[21] Ibid

ultimate, but just some characteristics that basically sum up pertinent traits.

Character

We may be able to compensate for the lack of experience, skills or education in many areas of leadership. But deficiencies in character will contradict our message and undermine our credibility. Real character is not the protection of innocence but the practice of virtue. This inner dynamic sparks contagious confidence. People receive the things of the Kingdom not only by what they hear; they must see it and experience it as well. They experience it in their leaders.

It has been said that almost 70% of leaders who successfully climb the ladder of leadership influence do not finish as expected. Some fail because of scandals and some just fade into obscurity. They fall short because in their outwardly successful lives there is a disconnection between the development competencies and the leadership character. However, the lack of character is the frequent cause of leaders failing to fulfill their true potential.

The New Testament church places great emphasis on character as the absolute pre-requisite.

1 Corinthians 4:17 reads:

"For this reason I am sending you Timothy, my son whom I love, who is faithful in the Lord. He will remind you of my way of life in Christ Jesus, which agrees with what I teach everywhere in every church."

The majority of Paul's requirement for elders and deacons, in his letter to Timothy, has to do with personal integrity and character. He says that Elders and Deacons must be "above reproach, the husband of one wife, temperate, prudent, respectable, hospitable, gentle, uncontentious, free from the love of money" (I Timothy 3:2-3). All of these words express important character qualities.[22]

You can lead without character, but character is what makes you a leader worth following. Your character will determine what people associate with your name. Gifting may determine your potential, but character will determine your legacy. Character is the will to do what is right even when it is hard.[23]

Apart from instructing Timothy, Paul also admonishes Titus who had the responsibility to appoint elders throughout Crete.

Titus 1:5-9 Reads:

"This is why I left you in Crete, that you might amend what was defective, and appoint elders in every town as I directed you, if any man is blameless, the husband of one wife, and his children are believers and not open to the charge of being profligate or insubordinate. For a bishop, as God's steward, must be blameless; he must not be arrogant or quick tempered or a drunkard or violent or greedy for gain, but hospitable, a lover of goodness, master of himself, upright, holy, and self- controlled; he must hold firm to the sure word as taught, so that he may be able to give instruction in sound doctrine and also to confute those who contradict it."

Character is about *will,* because it requires the willingness to make tough decisions. Sometimes, these decisions are contrary to emotions, intuition, economics, current trends and even common sense. Essentially character involves doing what is right because it's the right thing to do – regardless of the cost. We live in an environment where progress seems to call for compromise of conviction. But the still small voice that lurks inside will always, almost audible, blurt out – "this is wrong". Attention and adherence to this voice will make

---

[22] Rinehart Stacy – Upside down – NavPress – Colorado - 1998

[23] Stanley Andy – The Next Generation Leader – Colorado - 2003

the difference. Lack thereof will undermine every other trait, capability and potential. This includes accomplishments and accolades.

In Galatians 5:22-23, Paul lists nine items that sums up Godly character. Paul refers to these as the fruit of the Spirit – love, joy, peace, patience, kindness, goodness, faithfulness, gentleness and self-control.

Once again, it is rare that all of these qualities will be seen in any particular individual. Not impossible, but rare. Jesus displayed all of these attributes. Collectively, as a group of leaders, there is no reason where all of these cannot be evident, even though, dominant in some, more than others.

Authenticity

Webster's gives a definition of authenticity worthy of significant consideration. It says that authenticity means "being actually and precisely what is claimed." Further, when someone or something is authentic, it is authoritative because it conforms to the original, reproducing essential features.[24]

The basis of true power in church leadership is the power of personal spiritual authenticity. Spiritual authenticity is the validity of the Word of God and the Spirit of God demonstrated in the lives of leaders. People who lack such authenticity should not be entrusted with authority or official positions in the church.[25]

Essentially, character is who you are when no one is looking. If my character is authentic, then it will be consistent with what I profess, even when no one is around. In-spite of the circumstances, I should be increasingly displaying His character qualities. This authenticity

---

[24] Ibid

[25] Means E James – Leadership in Christian Ministry – Grand Rapids - 1989

becomes extremely attractive as the beauty of Christ shines through my life.

Enthusiasm

This portrays, first and foremost, the primary trait of a leader. The attitude **"I want to be a leader"** creates a strong foundation for successful leadership. Therefore, enthusiasm is important. No one can instill much enthusiasm in anyone for something about which he himself is not enthusiastic. Enthusiasm is often displayed in the manner in which a leader carries out his or her duties. Unless a person feels convinced that the work they are doing brings value and satisfaction they can never consistently act as though they do. This quality is very evident. It is easy to detect a lack of enthusiasm. This will be detected by the attitude displayed in a person. The lack of enthusiasm has detrimental effects. It has a negative influence that seems to transfer to people under that particular leader with disastrous effects. Enthusiasm ignites inspiration. Inspiration ignites passion. Passion is contagious.

Without enthusiasm great plans can be subject to failure. With enthusiasm no task is to great and no opposition to too formidable.

However, there has to be a balance with zeal and knowledge. Without this balance we can become over enthusiastic. The church of Corinth is a typical example of this. Fortunately, the Apostle Paul was able to, in time, rein them in.

Courage

Courageous leaders are grounded in their beliefs. They have the ability to adjust behavior as and when necessary. They are composed and are always consistent, displaying proper emotional control in all situations, including crisis situations.

An outstanding example is Joshua. The wandering in the wilderness of the children of Israel was reaching finality. The promised land was visually within reach. At this time there was a transition process of the change of leadership from Moses to Joshua. Israel faced many challenges. This transition, the passing of the baton from Moses to Joshua was ordained by God. Hence, Joshua's leadership was affirmed by God.

Joshua 1:5-9 reads:

"No man shall be able to stand before you all the days of your life; as I was with Moses, so I will be with you; I will not fail you or forsake you. Be strong and of good courage; for you shall cause this people to inherit the land which I swore to their fathers to them. Only be strong and very courageous, being careful to do according to all the law which Moses my servant commanded you; turn not from it to the right hand or to the left, that you may have good success wherever you go. This book of the law shall not depart out of your mouth, but you shall meditate on it day and night, that you may be careful to do according to all that is written in it; for then you shall make your way prosperous, and then you shall have good success."

Jesus re-affirmed this directive to his disciples in Matthew 28:20.

Never has there been a story of a man told greater than that of David. He epitomized the true example of a new generation leader.

There was a military stalemate between the army of Saul and the army of the Philistines. Nobody in the army of Saul was prepared or even contemplated being a hero, especially, when their opponent was Goliath.

1 Samuel 17:10-11 reads:

Again the Philistine said, "I defy the ranks of Israel this day; give me a man that we may fight together." When Saul and all of Israel heard these words of the Philistine, they were dismayed and greatly afraid.

Saul, together with his combat hardened veterans, were consumed with fear. David turns up to deliver lunch to his brothers who were in Saul's army. David's courage surpassed all of his physical evidence.

In fact, Saul and his army found Goliath too big to hit, while David found Goliath too big to miss.

Leadership takes courage. Leaders face problems in every aspect during the execution of their duties. Problems cannot, and will not go away. They have to be confronted and dealt with consistently. A courageous leader will deal with all problems as though they are challenges. Courage is not the absence of fear, courage assumes and consumes fear. This is handled with a sense of great joy. As long as we are dealing with people – there will always be challenges which require great courage to keep a sane mind!

Courage in leadership may take many different and unexpected forms. It may mean standing up for a principle and also mean having the character to stand up for what a person believes in without compromising ethics and values. A courageous leader will always remain loyal to their convictions.

Another challenge a leader is often faced with is managing upwards. This will take a lot of courage. Often times, we are managed by seniors who have little or no idea, or even a grasp, of the concepts or principles of leadership, especially if they are autocratic in their leadership styles, as most seniors generally are. Junior leaders often back down, due to various reasons, mostly intimidation.

Often times senior leaders' ideas and directions are the ultimate and it seems as though, God has only spoken to them because they would always start with the expression "the Lord showed me." Standing up with respect, to this type of leader takes great courage. Always remember in doing this, there are risks involved. Nevertheless do it anyway, providing you have sound reasons. Courage to act will define a leader, and this initiative will give those around him courage to follow, provided that you have sound reasons. However, this must be done with absolute temperament and respect. Courage is an establishing factor of leadership.

Self-confidence

This is also an important requirement, especially in making decisions concerning people. A leader has to be confident about himself in that he has the ability to make accurate decisions based on knowledge, facts and experience, not excluding wise counsel or advice. He has to be able to work with his personal assets and limitations.[26] He has to also understand his limitations. He must be willing to listen to other's opinions, assess them, and be mature enough to adopt the meritorious ones even if they do not square with his original thinking.

A self-confident leader is never satisfied with his accomplishments. He always sets about realizing his immediate and realistic goals. He always needs to stay ahead or abreast.

People who lead must know where they are going. They must demonstrate extraordinary levels of perception. Leaders need to have the ability of great inner strength and emotional stability. They must inspire confidence in others to want to follow them.[27]

Integrity

Integrity is the integration of lifestyles and belief so that they become one. It is also the uprightness of character and soundness of moral principles. This activates the inner dynamics that encourages others to follow with confidence.

Proverbs 11:3 reads

> **"The integrity of the upright guides them, but the unfaithful are destroyed by their duplicity."**

Proverbs 10:9 reads

> **"The man of integrity walks securely, but he who takes crooked paths will be found out"**

---

[26] Stafford John – Effective Management – Heinemann London – 1987

[27] Gibbs Eddie – Leadership next – intervarsity press – UK - 2005

Unless leaders are perceived to be people of outstanding integrity they cannot lead for long. If leaders lack integrity, they will be revealed eventually for what they really are: manipulators, power grabbers, or exploiters. They will eventually be rejected by their followers.[28]

1Timothy 3 and Titus 1 also discuss the issue of elder qualifications. Consistency of character and the presence of integrity are the measure of true leadership. It is important to look at the whole life, not just the ministry life. There must be a display of the character of Christ, which is integrity and authenticity.

A leader keeps his promise to both his team and to his superiors. He also keeps his promises made to himself, which are the most difficult to keep, and failure in this is the easiest to rationalize. He can keep all these promises because he never commits himself rashly, but always within the limits of reality and his present capabilities and in terms of his personal ability.[29]

Part of this matter of integrity is certain, unquestioned loyalty to his organization – to its reputation as well as his own. Loyalty to ones associates is extremely important in any leader. Part of his loyalty is a sense of stewardship – a feeling of responsibility for the welfare, progress and security of the organization as a whole and that of everyone who is a part of the organization and also to his family.

Nothing erodes a leader's effectiveness more than when his integrity is questioned. Reputation will make or break a leader. Leaders are called to act with integrity more than they are called to success.[30] Trust comes first. Leaders will gain the support of followers when they have proven that they can be trusted.

---

[28] Means E James – Leadership in Christian Ministry – Grand Rapids - 1989

[29] Stafford John – Effective Management – Heinemann - London - 1987

[30] Bob Briner & Ray Pritchard – Leadership Lessons of Jesus – Broadman & Holman – 1997

Your position will prompt people to lend you their hands. But, your integrity will inspire them to lend you their hearts.

It is integrity that will enable people to buy into a leader's vision.

Humility

Hebrews 13: 17 reads:

> **"Obey your leaders, and submit to them; for they keep watch over your souls, as those who will give an account. Let them do this with joy and not with grief, for this will be unprofitable for you."**

This verse is often quoted with regard to spiritual leadership. The Greek word for "submit" is hupeiko. This is its only appearance in the New Testament. The word can be translated here as "yield", "give way", or "be persuaded by." In the context of Hebrew, "be persuaded by" fits best because leaders who spoke the Word of God urged the Hebrews to imitate their faith, and therefore, to be persuaded by their speaking and by their lives. Submission here conveys the idea of allowing oneself to be influenced deeply by the word and life of a leader whose character is consistent and evident.[31]

One of the greatest attributes of a leader that somewhat seems to have a positive response toward people is humility. More often people respond to leaders because of their gentle and humble way of leading. Their character often persuades them of his spirituality. Humbleness portrays a godly example.

In other words, a sterling character, a growing intimacy, authenticity, integrity and humility – these are core qualifications of leadership. These are fruits budding from a long incubation period, rooted in the hidden places, manifesting themselves first in small places.[32]

---

[31] Rinehart Stacy – Upside down – NavPress – Colorado - 1998

[32] Ibid

Small things are the genuinely big things in the Kingdom of God. It is here, we truly face the issues of obedience and discipleship. It is not hard to be a model disciple amid camera lights and press releases. But, in the small corners of life, in those areas of service that will never be newsworthy or gain us any recognition, we must hammer out the meaning of obedience.[33]

A leader is not necessarily evaluated by his position, achievements, theological training, or natural abilities. Traits like self- control, humility, and faithfulness becomes the barometer of one's fitness to lead. True leaders reflect to those around them, the character of Christ as they know Him internally.

Hebrews 1:3 reads:

> **"The Son is the radiance of God's glory and the exact representation of his being, sustaining all things by His powerful word. After he had provided purification for sins, he sat down at the right hand of the Majesty in heaven."**

Jesus' claims and the way He lived were in agreement. This should describe a spiritual leader. His word and life must match up.

The heart of spiritual leadership is serving people with great humility, looking out for what is best for them. Therefore, the question that should not be asked is – "Does the leader have followers?" but rather "Does the Lord have followers through the leader's influence?"

Paul encouraged Timothy to aspire to be a leader, not because leadership only represents authority, but a position of service.

Mark 10: 42-44 reads:

> **"Jesus called them together and said, you know that those who are recognized as rulers of the Gentiles lord it over them; and their great men exercise authority over**

---

[33] Foster J Richard – Celebration of Discipline – Harper and Row – 1978

them. But it is not so among you, but whoever wishes to become great among you shall be your servant; and whoever wishes to be first among you shall be slave to all."

Jesus draws clear distinction between the paradigms of leadership. In doing so he defines with clarity, giving direction on the style to adopt.

This best explains the attitude of Jesus and the example he set for leaders to follow. His strength of rule was from a position and posture of humility.

Relationship

Relationship is the ability of people to enjoy a sense of closeness, in some instances, intertwining which may result in interdependence. It is also a form of kinship. However, there has to be a balance between too far and too close. The happy medium can only be determined by those involved in that specific relationship.

This is not an option based on choice. A leader cannot choose to lead from afar. Neither should he choose a hermit's attitude based on confinement or separation. There has to be some level of interaction without missing the important ingredient, relationship.

God gave Moses Ten Commandments on Mount Sinai. These commandments have a two pronged approach. The first being commandments one to five, and the second being commandments six to ten. The first five commandments give us an indication of the emphasis God placed on service to Himself.

The second set of five commandments gives us an indication of the emphasis placed on service to one another. Hence, the entire set of Ten Commandments is based purely, on relationship to God and people. These are intertwined and therefore, complement each other. These cannot be isolated from each other. Simply put, we cannot have a relationship with God without having a relationship with each other.

Mark 12: 28-31 reads:

> *One of the teachers of the law came and heard them debating. Noticing that Jesus had given them a good answer, he asked him, "of all the commandments, which is the most important?'*
>
> **"The most important one," answered Jesus, "is this: 'Hear O Israel, the Lord our God, the Lord is one. Love the Lord your God with all your heart and with all your soul and with all your mind and with all your strength.' The second is this: 'Love your neighbor as yourself.' There is no commandment greater than these."**

In these verses of scripture, Jesus gives a summary of the commandments God gave to Moses. He summed it up with just two statements: **"Love the Lord your God and Love your neighbor as yourself."**

Christ typifies a new basis of relationship, not based as that depicted by Nehemiah as being charged with the task of discerning God's mind for His people and then instructing everyone accordingly. Jesus instituted an order based on mutuality and interdependence.

Often times Jesus would command – **love one another – serve one another – put one another first** – the list goes on. Jesus portrays a view of leadership based on a relational context.

Jesus also inaugurated a new basis of relationship for leaders.

Matthew 28:8 reads:

> **"But you are not to be called 'Rabbi,' for you have only one Master and you are all brothers."**

John 15:15 reads:

> **"I no longer call you servants, because a servant does not know his master's business. Instead, I have called**

friends, for everything I learned from my Father I have made known to you."

Relationship in His kingdom does not exist on a hierarchical basis, with someone being over one person and under one another. Rather, we stand and fall together, shoulder to shoulder, brothers and sisters in a common spiritual family.[34]

Christ transcended the human barriers that would normally divide and separate us as individuals – race, gender, and background.[35]

Colossians 3:11 reads:

"Here there is no Greek or Jew, circumcised or uncircumcised, barbarian, Scythian, slave or free, but Christ is all, and is in all."

Relationships are the basic blocks of His kingdom. Core functions of leadership must be relational in nature. To violate the basic relational nature of the body is to transgress the bounds of spiritual leadership. When we violate this irreducible minimum, we reveal that our leadership concept comes not from the Spirit but from the world around us.[36]

In many church organizations, leaders are treated as employees. Leaders in turn, treat other members as laborers. This gives rise to structures within the organization that leads to a power model rather than a relationship model.

Competence

This is the ability of a person to possess the adequacy, skills, capacity, knowledge and qualification to perform given tasks or to execute duties as prescribed to agreed standards. To be competent is to acquisition knowledge, skills, abilities and expertise to perform in an

---

[34] Rinehart Stacy – Upside down – NavPress – Colorado - 1998
[35] Rinehart Stacy – Upside down – NavPress – Colorado - 1998
[36] Ibid

appropriate setting, within inside or outside academia. This is the ability to work consistently and also to transfer skills.

This is a tough call or a tall order for recruitment. We can argue as to whether this is necessary, or important in a selection of a leader. For a moment, think of how the corporate world functions. Whenever a position is advertised, core competences are listed as guidelines to ensure the selection of the best possible candidate. Meaning that, the person that comes closest to meeting the criteria regarding these competencies is eligible for recruitment.

If this is the view of the corporate world, in ensuring that the best talent is explored, why then do we lower our standards?

Having said this, there is a flip side to the coin. Unfortunately, we may not necessarily have the talents and expertise to fit the profile we require. Hence, we use whatever limited resources available to us. Herein lies the significance of training and development. This must be a continuous process, also used for succession planning.

In our earnest endeavors to find competent leaders, there must be balance of requirements versus the eligible candidate. Meaning that, certain competencies are absolutely necessary. For example, a leader that is not academically inclined cannot lead a group of university graduates or for that matter, a person who has no patience with children cannot lead a children's group etc.

Vision

This somewhat encompasses and defines the sum total of, or a leader in totality. Vision is an interpretation and practical application of a God given imagination. In a spiritual realm, vision helps leaders to see with an eye of faith. We become purpose driven, with a sense of destiny. We see the end for which the beginning was created. However, it must not be confused with imagination!!

I had the wonderful opportunity of visiting Disney World in Orlando, Florida. I also had the opportunity to be part of group that enjoyed a "behind the scenes" tour of Disney World. We were given lots of information on what actually happens behind the scenes. Several thousand visit Disney World monthly and enjoy the great rides and scenic beauty of fairy tales brought to reality. They are oblivious of what goes on behind the scenes, the work, effort, precision and demonstration of excellence that brings insurmountable mind boggling experiences to those that visit.

One of the most amazing theme parks I visited is called EPCOT – **Electronic Prototype of the Community of Tomorrow**. Both my mind and imagination could not contain, or explain how this place came into being. It was an out of the world experience, that up to this day – several years later, I cannot comprehend how this theme park became a reality. I still marvel in amazement, as to how such an extraordinary vision was brought to reality – not just reality but brought to life.

The tour guide also gave us some useful information of the history of Disney World and how it was started by Walt Disney. I suppose if you google Disney World this information can be obtained. But, being there, first hand, was indeed, an experience of a life time. The most amazing feature was the vision of one person that brought to life a "dream world" that is an international attraction. Walt Disney did see some of the theme parks, not only in vision but in reality. The Tour guide mentioned that Walt Disney died before EPCOT was a reality. Hence, he never got to see it.

But alas!! I beg to differ. Walt Disney saw it before he died. That is how it became a reality. He was a visionary. EPCOT existed in Walt Disney's mind. He had a vision which ultimately gave birth to reality.

Vision arises out of a clear sense of purpose. It is not just a bright idea or a success guaranteed option. It originates out of our God given imagination, resulting in incubation and eventually the expression of the mind of God. Vision inspires us to reach heights we never deemed possible or imaginable. As leaders we become principal advocates and guardians of the fulfilment of the vision with clarity and conviction. We can delay God but cannot deny God. God will raise a generation of leaders who will bring to fruition that which He has planned and purposed before the foundations of the earth. Leaders today, have to be able to carry that Prophetic Declaration and ensure that they have the ability to access the realms of the Spirit and bring down that which has been declared by the prophets. Therefore, while we have our own personal vision and agendas or imaginations, the vision of leadership flows out of the mission of a God-given mandate.

Vision must be owned, shaped and articulated by the culture of what God is doing in a particular household of faith. Visions are larger than a leader. Leaders are merely custodians of a vision. While line leaders prioritize key issues and engage with finer details, the leader ensures that focus on the completion or fruition of the vision which never grows dim. In a spiritual sense, we live and breathe – we become one with the vision. We become the subject matter of the vision. By virtue of communicating, the Vision becomes contagious. Obviously, this has to be based on divine revelation. People will not respond to manipulative, self-serving, egocentric and power hungry types of vision. People will respond when visions stem out of passion, commitment, enthusiasm and more important, that which emanates out of the Throne Room of God. This is void of rationality, analysis and impossibilities.

These are highly significant, core, basic fundamentals that reflect leadership qualities. People who exhibit these behaviors and attitudes tend to attract followers. Followers have a tendency to be drawn to leaders that can inspire belief in them. However, no single person is gifted with all of these traits. Hence, there is no reason to live in a myth that such a super person exists. There is, also, no reason to feel inadequate when we measure ourselves against this list. However, as an entire leadership team we will complement each other. Our strength, weakness and challenges create an even playing field as a team of leaders. We are able to draw from one another's resources and expertise. Society does place a high premium on individuals who have the responsibility to lead others.

There is an old adage that states, "don't do what I do, do as I tell you to." This is a blatant disregard for the authenticity and sincerity, epitomized by Jesus.

In John 13:1-17, Jesus provides a perfect example that negates this adage with vigor. He became the perfect servant leader washing the feet of his team of leaders.

If the basic principles of these qualities are understood, a fair idea of a profile of a leader can be easily determined. These qualities, even though, may vary from each other, are not negotiable nor can be adjusted to suit circumstances or situations or even personal profiles or agendas. These cannot be learned, but can be developed, unlike skills. These are inherent qualities that should be easily identified in anyone who aspires to be a leader. They either have it or do not. This is the point where there is great controversy to the argument as to whether leaders are born or made. The ultimate measurement is the ability to change or influence current and future generations.

Basically, those who choose to follow want to be sure that a leader is worth following. They will judge, not so much for where they are lead, but how they are lead. They will sum up, not only the leader's skills but also leader's value as a person. There is a significant difference between having a following and being worthy of following. The leader's entire life is put under a microscope.

Character, loyalty, support, etc. are irrelevant. In the final analysis, it is what you want to be remembered for, the type of legacy you want to leave behind, that is important. The legacy of a leader is not based on longevity, but activity.

Chapter 4

Know Thyself

These were the wise word of Socrates.

There is another dimension to knowing thyself – As others know you. There is often, a dichotomy when an attempt is made on the basis of self-analysis. Often times, there are distinct differences between knowing yourself and as others know you. This multiple personality profile must cease to exist. There should always be a mirror image of knowing thyself, and as others know you. Sometimes, when certain incidents come to knowledge, there is often an element of surprise. Certain aspects or actions of a person's behavior cannot be believed. We have difficulty in associating an incident or behavior with a particular person we know. Simply, because we know them, or rather we think we know them, differently. I can think of many examples of unexpected behavior displayed by certain people. How often have we surprised ourselves? We have, sometimes, done or said things that we could not believe we actually did.

To know oneself is to have the ability or the capability of being aware and understanding your personal limitations and core competencies. However, we are often encouraged to think and act beyond limitations and barriers that can be seen, in the natural. In the spiritual realm, we need to think beyond the capacity of our mind in order to be able to, not only overcome and live victoriously, but lead effectively. This requires us to exercise our faith in God and on His Word. However, while this is positive and adds a different dimension in our thinking perspective, we must not lose sight of the fact that we have limitations. We must not, and should not, confuse faith with wisdom. We must admit that certain tasks and challenges stretch beyond our abilities and competencies. Every person has strengths and weaknesses. It is of absolute necessity that leaders realize they are unable to achieve all things. This brings to light one of the fundamentals as to why leadership should function as a team. This gives room to balance out our strengths and weaknesses. Invariably, often times, one's weakness will be someone else's strength and vice versa.

So, we must accept that we have limitations. There are some things we can accomplish, some things we strive to accomplish and some things we will never be able to accomplish, even if we tried. This is totally dependent on our ability to know ourselves, and work within the confines of our limitations. This is not an indictment on our capabilities or competencies. There is always a temptation to pretend to know more that we really do. We feel that we need to portray the image that expresses a certain level of intelligence. This will definitely, give room for personal discouragement and disappointments in the long term. Therefore, we need to be able to operate within the confines of our limitations, provided we give of our best at all times.

There is a huge difference between opportunity and obligations. As leaders, we want to be able to do more than is required of us. But, we have to face reality. Failure to face reality is called denial. Denial leads to unhealthy relationships. "Nobody can know you, like you know yourself." Therefore, no matter how we feel about our ego and self-esteem, we have a limited capacity. We cannot be all things to all people.

For the purposes of self-analysis, to know and understand the different dimensions of behaviour, I have used a scientifically proven psychological theory called the Johari Window.

The Johari window is a behavioral model created by psychologists, Joseph Luft and Harry Lingham in 1955. The name Johari is derived from the combination of both the names of the psychologists. This model primary deals with self-awareness. This is an excellent point of reference for the analysis of one's psychological profile. This brings to light, not only a sense of awareness, but, some startling information if attempted with absolute honesty.

The Johari Window shows four dimensions of selfhood found in every person.[37]

1. My public life is the part of me that is known to others.
2. My blind self is known to others but not to me.
3. My private life is known to me but unknown to others.
4. My unknown self is hidden from both me and others.

Johari Window Model

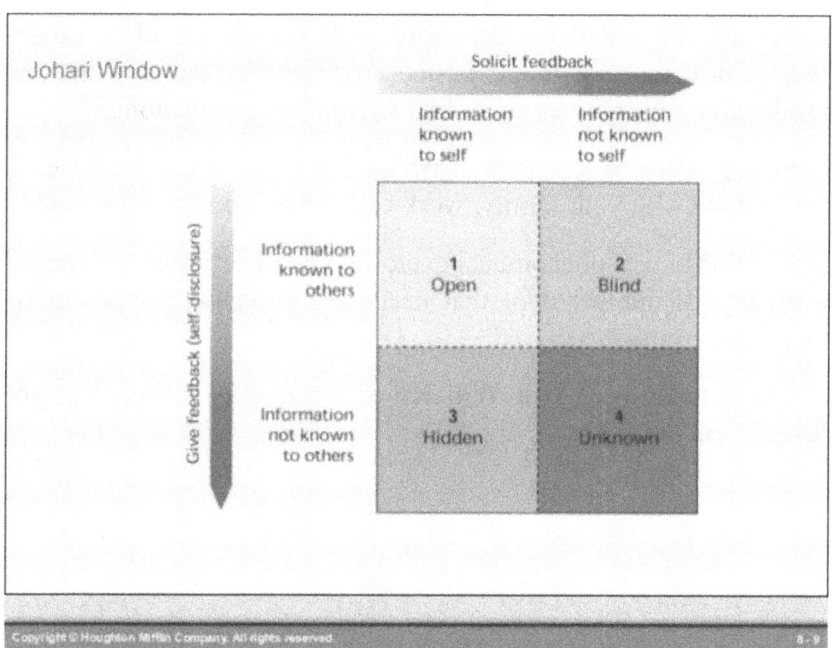

Quadrant 1 – **The Open Area** – refers to behavior and motivation known to self and others. It shows the extent to which two or more

---

[37] Hersey P and Blanchard K – Organisational Behaviour – New Jersey -1977

persons can freely give and take, work together and enjoy experiences together. The larger this area, the greater people's contact with reality and the more open are their abilities and needs to themselves and their associates.

Quadrant 2 – **The Blind area** – represents behavior and motivation not known to people themselves but which are readily apparent to others.

Quadrant 3 – **The Hidden Area** – means behavior and motivation open to the person but kept secret from others. Some call this quadrant the hidden agenda.

Quadrant 4 – **Area of Unknown Activity** – means behavior and motivation not known to the individuals themselves or to others. People know this quadrant exists because they occasionally discover new behavior or motives never known, but present all along.[38]

There are different scenarios to which this exercise can be done. It can be done with your family, work colleagues, church groups etc.

I found this to be a phenomenal exercise. The results bring awareness to aspects of our behavior that needs adjustments, changes or re-alignment.

The final analysis – **You Will Know Yourself** – better than you thought you did.

---

[38] D'Souza Anthony – Leadership – Paulines Publications - 2003

Chapter 5

Theories of Motivation

After discovering "Know Thyself", it is important to establish what motivates you or more important, what generally motivates anyone. There are several arguments based on different perceptions and circumstances about what actually motivates people.

The word motivation is derived from the word motive. The Oxford dictionary suggests two definitions of this word: the reason for something, and productive of motion. Hence, the basic definition could be – that which impels a person to action.

The simple conclusion as to why we want people motivated is that if they are motivated the desired results are often achieved. As leaders, it is our responsibility to ensure that people are constantly motivated. This is not an easy task as working with people can be very difficult at times. Remember, people are emotional beings.

On a frequent basis, we read about various motivational speakers asking people to attend their sessions. People are promised, and in some cases, guaranteed total satisfaction in marriage, some promise quick get rich schemes, some guarantee total mind satisfaction, and the list goes on. People that respond to these sessions often return with a great sense of motivation and determination. As time passes, like most things in life, this hyped sense of motivation seems to slowly fade away. People generally revert back to their original lifestyle. There always seem to be a gravitational pull toward the status quo. Generally, the confusion is that instead of motivation, a lot of excitement is generated. Hence, fading away is the result.

The same argument applies to money. Many will argue that money is a motivator. This is not the case. When someone is promoted and given an increase or finds better employment with higher salaries, they are highly motivated. This does not last for more than a while before there is a need for more. No amount of money will be ever enough. The theory of 'the more we have the more we want" will always be there to remind us that enough is never enough, especially money.

The same applies to our Christian life. We are often motivated by a sermon we have just heard, a conference or a youth camp we have attended, or even a leadership seminar conference. We return highly motivated and as time goes by this motivation seems to slowly fade away. Even when desperate prayers are answered, we promise God all sorts of commitments. Once again, as time goes by, this motivation slowly dwindles. A good example of this is New Year's resolutions. We even convince ourselves that we will keep our resolutions. Before the year is out, we are just the same as we entered into it. Very seldom, does the same level of motivation last, and we actually keep our commitments or resolutions.

So then, what motivates people?

Motivation consists of both internal and external factors. What we have discussed thus far, are external factors. External factors border mostly on excitement. This does not last. If, by chance it does, it is very rare.

Internal factors have a more lasting or permanent influence. We must understand that genuine motivation comes from within. Leaders, or those that aspire to be leaders, have to understand what motivates people.

Before we look at some scientific and psychological aspects, based on research from some of the world's greatest authorities on this subject, I cannot help but think of Nehemiah. His handling of the situation in Jerusalem illustrates for us the essence of great motivation. For ninety years, the people had been saying "it cannot be done" (the rebuilding of the wall). Under Nehemiah there is a united and enthusiastic effort to work together and rebuild the wall. All of this is as a result of great and inspired leadership. Nehemiah had the ability to motivate the people and bring to completion the rebuilding of the wall.

The basis of knowing people is understanding people!

What are their concerns and needs? What are the key drivers that keep them ticking? What is our understanding of human motivation – not everything is about being spiritual. The realities are that we are human, and have serious basic needs like shelter, food, etc. which needs to be satisfied before any level of motivation is evident. Many have difficulties just to make ends meet. We cannot expect everybody to be at the same level of motivation. The key is to understand what people are motivated by before trying in vain to motivate them. For the purposes of understanding key components, I have used some scientific psychological models that are relevant to us today.

Maslow's Theory

The late Professor Abraham Maslow was known as the father of modern motivational thought. He set out a five stage priority of human needs in what has become known as Maslow's Pyramid or Maslow's hierarchy of needs. This gives us a broad concept of understanding human motivation.

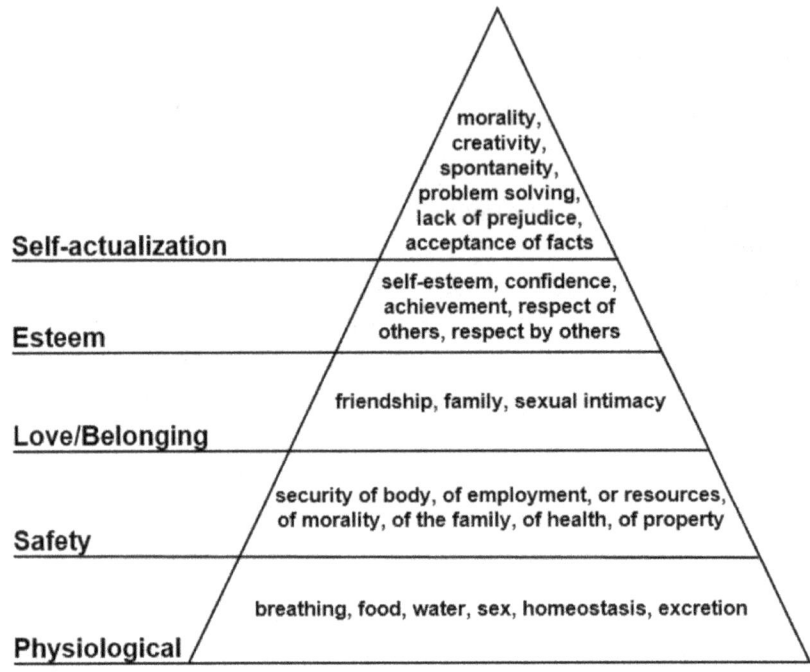

The basis of this theory is that the bottom level is prime, in that a person who is starving because of the lack of food or water will be unconcerned about anything else until those needs are satisfied. However, they are no more important than any other level, since each of us will be motivated only by the *lowest unfulfilled need*.[39] For Example, when someone has just had a meal, the offer of food will not motivate, since that person will have moved on to the second level, the need to be safe and feel secure.

Biological and Physiological Needs

Basic life needs, air, food, drink, shelter, warmth, sleep etc.

Level one, in a nutshell, can be referred to as economic empowerment, which influences everything we do. It defines both our destiny and our legacy. Within this level is embedded our dignity,

---

[39] Strafford John – Effective Management – Heinemann– London - 1987

as it is one of the foundations of our existence. True liberation does not originate from political freedom, but from economic emancipation.

Safety Needs

Protection, security, order, law, limits, stability etc.

The second level applies to safety from physical attacks, and a reassurance which could mean job security, shelter etc. If we feel safe and secure then another level affects us.

This level can also be referred to as the political component of our lives. It has to do with having some sort of input in the political system. Meaning that we have influence in both government and governance.

Belongingness and Love Needs

Family, affection, relationship, work etc.

The next level applies to our social needs. We need love, friendship and a feeling of belonging. We need to be a part of a family and also a group of our peers.

This component can also be termed as restitution, that is, when people give back to society when their physical and security needs are met. This can lead to mental empowerment. This is the ability to think beyond the capacity of our minds and the boundaries prescribed by society within our limitations.

Esteem Needs

Achievements, status, responsibility, reputation etc.

The next level of need is self-esteem. This is the need for self-respect and to be respected by others. According to Maslow, this need can be classified into two sets:

First, Maslow speaks about the desire for strength, for achievement, for adequacy, for confidence to face the world, and for independence and freedom.

Secondly, one's desire for reputation or prestige (defined as respect or esteem for other people), recognition, importance, attention or appreciation.[40]

Self Actualization

Personal growth and fulfilment etc.

If all needs for esteem are satisfied, the individual is then motivated by the highest need, self- actualization, which is the desire to make full use of one's own abilities and talents. In other words, if all the lower needs are satisfied (and this only occurs in a small portion of us), people begin to function with the best of their abilities.

A person may not remain in one level for a long time. People can relatively move to different levels within a very short space of time depending on the satisfaction of their needs.

Maslow does not tell us how to satisfy these needs. We have to depend on our basic human sense and act accordingly. For example, if a person is starving, we must offer them food. It is difficult when we are considering safety, social or esteem needs.

However, the ultimate of mental freedom is spiritual empowerment. This is a higher dimension which looks on higher needs beyond the body and mind. It is extremely difficult to think of mental or spiritual empowerment if basic needs are unfulfilled. These are stark realities that cannot be ignored. A holistic approach is necessary to a ascertain input and output measurements in both leaders and those they lead.

The leader cannot motivate someone to express full potential (level 4) if they are having family problems.

---

[40] Strafford John – Effective Management – Heinemann– London - 1987

A leader cannot expect to be a team leader (level 3) if they have difficulties paying their rent or bond (Level 2).

One cannot expect someone to turn up at all meetings if they have a challenge with level 2.

The list can go on – hence, a deeper understanding of people profiling is important as different people have challenges at different levels.

What is interesting is that organizations who genuinely care about, understand, encourages their people to self-actualization are the most successful organizations.

Herzberg's Theory

Professor Frederick Herzberg promoted a theory which is based on the reward system.

- What makes people happy and motivated is what they do.
- What makes people unhappy and de-motivated is the situation in which they do it.[41]

The quality of life plays an important part here. This starts by defining people as they are, not what we want them to be. People have to be treated and respected for who they are.

Is this asking too much?

Herzberg has suggested that these needs fall into two categories.

Hygiene needs – this relates to a person's relationship with the environment. How a person is treated has significant consequences as to how he will respond. Treat them like children and they will respond like children.[42]

---

[41] Ibid
[42] Ibid

Keep them in a controlled environment with autocratic style leadership, and they will respond with ignorance.

These are called hygiene factors because they prevent people from being dissatisfied or unhappy, which is their function, but they do not motivate. This has to also do with fair treatment. The lack of fair treatment is often never forgotten. In the introduction we spoke about this. This is one of the key weaknesses of leadership. People are made up of feelings and emotions and therefore have to be treated without impartiality. It is in the interest of the leader and organization that people are treated fairly.

Motivators - This is the second set of needs. People do not want to be hurt. They need to be treated well. They want to do something. They also want to show what they can do. The only way to measure this is by what they have done.[43]

Participation is a key role player here. This eliminates the "one man band" scenario. Team effort plays an important part here. Measurable tools must be put in place and constant progressive reports must be made to all showing achievement, strength and weaknesses. If these are put in place, people will respond with positive attitudes. Hurt seems to be a common denominator. Some have had to endure lasting pain, just because some leaders do not know how to bridle their tongues.

McGregor – The Theory of X And Y

Douglas McGregor suggested interest in people has a significant effect in motivating people. Most leaders believe in theory X, which means:

1. People are inherently lazy
2. They will not work unless they are forced to

---

[43] Ibid

3. They are not interested in and do not want to take responsibility

This is only true because of certain experiences and expectations a leader may have had. This perception ultimately brings out an autocratic style of management that demands subordination. Again, people respond by the way they are treated.

McGregor suggested that if leaders adopted theory Y, then people will respond better.

Common goals are shared between leader and team.

1. People are given responsibility and, therefore, contribute to the end result.
2. People are given the chance to develop their abilities.[44]

Again, the principle of expectation is applicable. If we expect people to be lazy, they will be lazy. On the other hand, if we expect people to contribute, they will contribute. The inference here is there must be greater acknowledgement of the reliability on people to produce as per expectation.

In *Pygmalion,* George Bernard Shaw's play, Eliza Dolittle explains to Freddie:

"You see, really and truly, apart from the things anyone can pick up (the dressing and the proper way of speaking, and so on) the difference between a lady and a flower girl is not how she behaves, but how she is treated. I shall always be a flower girl to Professor Higgins, because he always treats me as a flower girl, and always will; but I know I can be a lady to you, because you always treat me like as a lady, and always will."[45]

---

[44] Strafford John – Effective Management – Heinemann– London – 1987
[45] Shaw George Bernard –Pygmalion –quote by Anthony D'Souza – leadership – Paulines Publication 2003

The Pygmalion effect is more or less a self-fulfilling prophecy. Leaders are always influencing the behavior of others in some way through expectations and assumptions. People sometimes become what others expect of them. This further reinforces McGregor's principles based on theory Y.

The purpose of including Maslow, Herzberg and McGregor's theories is that we now have a scientific idea of what psychological and physiological components people are made up of and how to apply the level of motivation that pertains to the different levels of needs. It must be understood that we are human beings functioning as spiritual beings in a real world. People differ one from another and have to be managed and motivated according to their abilities and levels of understanding. This understanding between the leader and team creates a climate conducive to motivation. If this philosophy is inculcated, immeasurable results are achieved at greatly reduced stress levels.

Nothing can stand in the way of a motivated team. No mountain is too high, no valley is too deep, no current too strong, no task too difficult!

King David in the book of 1 Chronicles, Chapter 12 epitomized this!

Chapter 6

Communication

Introduction

From the beginning of time and creation, also since the book of Genesis, the greatest tragedy that befalls man is the lack of communication. This lack still continues to plague every aspect of our existence, from family life, vocational life to secular life. The lack of communication is the single most common cause of breakdown in marriages, family life and social circles, even the demise of organizations. Large companies and corporations have suffered huge losses, and in some cases liquidated, purely on the basis of failure to or lack of communication to customers, staff and shareholders.

This is further aggravated by the silence of man not having the ability to speak out in time, to avoid disaster. This passivity has resulted in destruction and disaster beyond measure. Here is a classic example.

The example of Adam

Genesis 2:15-22 reads:

> "The Lord God took the man and put him in the Garden of Eden to work it and take care of it.
>
> 16 – And the Lord God commanded the man, "you are free to eat from any tree in the garden;
>
> 17- but you must not eat from the tree of the knowledge of good and evil, for when you eat of it you will surely die."
>
> 18- The Lord God said, "It is not good for man to be alone. I will make a helper suitable for him."

> **19-** Now the Lord God had formed out of the ground all the beasts of the field and all the birds of the air. He brought them to the man to see what he would name them; and whatever the man called each living creature, that was its name.
>
> **20-** So the man gave names to all the livestock, the birds of the air and all the beasts of the field. But for Adam no suitable helper was found.
>
> **21-** So the Lord God caused man to fall into a deep sleep; and while he was sleeping, he took one of the man's ribs and closed up the place with flesh.
>
> **22-** Then the Lord God made a woman from the rib he had taken out of the man, and he brought her to the man."

"God created Adam, put him in the garden and specifically instructed him not to eat of the tree of knowledge and evil" – verse 17.

Genesis 3:6-7 reads:

> **"When the woman saw that the fruit of the tree was good for food and pleasing to the eye, and also desirable for gaining wisdom, she took some and ate it. She also gave some to her husband, who was with her, and he ate it.**
>
> **7-** Then the eyes of both of them were opened, and they realized they were naked; so they sewed fig leaves together and made coverings for themselves."

Note that in verse 6 – when Eve ate of the fruit – she gave some to her husband who was with her at that time, and he ate it

Picture the scene - Satan was having a conversation with Eve about the forbidden fruit. Satan eventually convinces Eve to eat the forbidden fruit. Eve eats and then offers to Adam. Adam also eats of the forbidden fruit.

Adam was there during the entire episode between Eve and Satan. He did not do or say anything to Eve or satan, in-spite of God giving him specific instructions not to eat of the forbidden fruit. He was created by God first and was given delegated authority. Adam was given the ability to create and speak order out of disorder. In Genesis 1:3 God Spoke and in Genesis 2:19-20 man spoke. Therefore, Adam was, or should have been in charge here, not Eve or Satan. He literally failed to act as a leader. He failed to take charge of the situation at hand. He said, or did, absolutely nothing by choice. Instead, he had the audacity to eat of the forbidden fruit.

Genesis 3: 8-12 reads:

> **"Then the man and his wife heard the sound of the Lord God as he was walking in the garden in the cool of the day, and they hid from the Lord God among the trees of the garden.**
>
> **9- But the Lord God called to the man, "Where are you?"**
>
> **10-he answered, "I heard you in the garden, and I was afraid because I was naked; so I hid.**
>
> **11- And he said, "who told you that you were naked? Have you eaten from the tree that I commanded you not to eat from?'**
>
> **12- The man said, "the woman you put here with me – she gave me some fruit for the tree, and I ate it."**

God called out to Adam – verse 10. This further indicates that Adam was in charge or accountable. God asked Adam if he had eaten of the forbidden fruit – verse 11. Here again, God was addressing Adam. Adam responded – **"the woman you put here with me"** in verse-12 gave me the fruit. He indirectly blamed God in verse 12, because God had given him the woman.

This is a classic case of a breakdown in communication on the part of Adam. He had the authority to communicate, to both Eve and Satan, the instruction that God had given him. He should have intervened and challenged Satan about his sudden concern for both him and Eve. Despite having a God-given authority he failed to restrain both Eve and Satan. His failure to communicate with authority resulted in a disaster, with great consequences, which has affected the world to this day.

The Example of Abraham

God made a promise to Abraham that he would have a son and be a father of a multitude, through whom God will bless the world – (Gen 15). After ten years, and no children, Sarah tells Abraham to take her slave Hagar, and have children with her so that God's promise can come to pass. Genesis 16:2 tells us that Abraham listened to Sarah. He failed to take charge of the situation as a leader of the house and to remind Sarah of the promise God had made to them. This was not how God had intended for the promise to be fulfilled. This was later emphasized in Genesis 17:16 the message was clear – **"and I will bless her (Sarah) and give you a son also of her (Sarah) – I will bless her (Sarah) and she shall be a mother (Sarah) of nations; kings of people shall be of her (Sarah)."**

After Ishmael was born, Sarah became envious. She felt that she had failed to produce a son. This led to a feeling of inferiority. There was animosity in the household. Abraham, for the fear of not keeping Sarah happy, tells her to do what she wants to Hagar who was ultimately her slave. Sarah treated Hagar harshly. Hagar was subsequently banished with Ishmael. Because of the communication problem between Abraham and Sarah, the effects of the Arab/Israeli conflict still rage on today.

The Example of Lot

In the book of 2 Peter 2:7, we learn that Lot was a righteous man. We would not have known this from the account in Genesis. He stayed in Sodom and Gomorrah and was silent about the evil around him.

At the end of the account when they are fleeing the city, Lot's wife looks back at Sodom and turns into a pillar of salt. If Lot was tormented in his soul by the evil around him (2 Peter 2:8), why then didn't he leave. It was obvious that his wife wanted to stay. He had a communication problem with his wife. He remained silent and passive.

There are several more examples in the Bible that clearly show the breakdown in communication with disastrous results. Often, objectives are not achieved; goals are not attained, this is due primarily to the breakdown in communication. This is also as a result of differences in views and perceptions. The failure to check understanding also contributes highly. Communication is an age old art that has never been perfected.

For better understanding, I think we need to look at the scientific, yet practical approach, with the view of knowing and learning how the whole concept of communication operates.

Levels of communication

There are five levels of communication that suggest an ever-deepening process of interaction in the communication between two people.[46]

1. *The cliché*

This level involves the social ritual which we use almost daily. An example of this is an exchange of greeting. When these greetings are exchanged, they are generally superficial. When you ask somebody how they are, they usually reply fine. In actual fact, they may not be fine. There is no factual value to this type of conversation except an exchange of greetings.

---

[46] Powell John – Why I am afraid to tell you who I am? – Tabor Publishing - 1969

2. *The reporting facts*

This level involves factual sharing of information about the weather, the children etc. This level of communication does not involve the individual or his opinions as they are unimportant.

3. *The beliefs and opinions*

This level involves a point of self-disclosure. This is when opinions and beliefs are expressed. When I communicate my beliefs about something, I am sharing who I am. If you disagree, I will feel that you are rejecting me.[47]

4. *The disclosure of feelings*

This level involves feeling safe enough with someone to tell them how you feel about something. This is generally associated with emotions. This is a risk as feelings can be rejected by someone else, especially, if there is a different view of the particular situation in question.

5. *The Peak*

This level involves a communication that knows no fear of rejection. Therefore, there is no need to fear communication of feelings. A person can share feelings with freedom and transparency.

The model of communication

Models are theories that help us to understand the whole process. It shows how communication takes place from source to completion – back to source. **For the purposes of this exercise the Shannon Weaver Model is used.**[48]

---

[47] Mitchell Costa – Intimacy in Marriage – Struikhof – Cape Town - 1991

[48] Abbey R Merril – communication in Pulpit and Parish – Westminster Press – Philadelphia – 1976

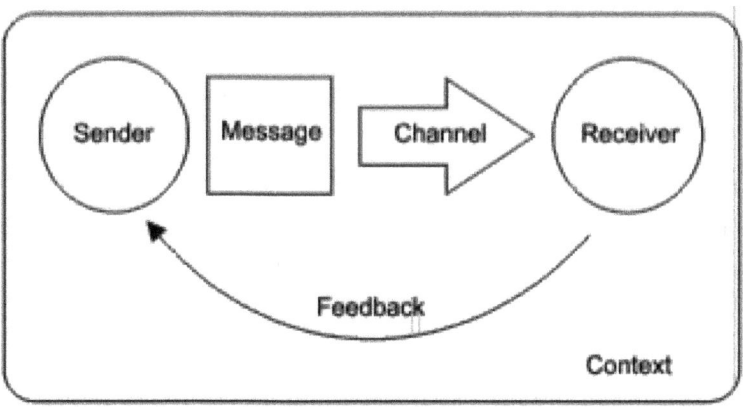

Process of Communication

Eddie Gibbs, in his book, Leadership Next, quotes Cloke and Goldsmith identifying key elements in communication.

- Encouraging: 'Please tell me more'
- Soliciting: Seek advice and clarification.
- Normalizing: 'Many people feel the way you do.'
- Acknowledging and empathizing: 'I can appreciate why you feel the way you do.'
- Mirroring: Reflect back the emotions and body language.
- Reframing: Reframe 'you' statements into 'I' statements.
- Summarizing: rephrase to test understanding.
- Validating: 'I appreciate your willingness'[49]

It is important to understand that communication is a circular process. Sending a message hoping that someone will understand it, is not communicating. Even if the message is heard by the receiver, it is not communication. Communication only takes place when a sender

---

[49] Gibbs Eddie – Leadership Next – Intervarsity Press – UK- 2005

sends a message, encoded in a form that can be decoded effectively by the receiver, who hears it, and responds to the sender with feedback to indicate that he has under stood the message.[50] It is necessary to restate accurately the content of what was relayed. Not only restate, but show understanding and respond accordingly.

A caring leader is an 'information collector' and also disseminator of information. He takes communication seriously. Decisions have to be made that sometimes effect people's lives. Wrong decisions can have detrimental repercussions.

This is an important and also an integral part of leadership. It is also vital to achieve maximum results. Breakdown in communication has caused much harm and will continue to do so, unless we get this simple formula right. One of the most popular grounds for divorce is breakdown in communication. One of the most popular reasons for the breakdown in family relationship and loss of family values is through the breakdown in communication. One of the prime reasons for wayward and disobedient children is the breakdown in communication. This list can go on, and I am sure that even as you think back, you will be able to relate to incidents in your own life, and also be able to quote examples of incidents where there has been a breakdown of communication.

In spite of all the modern technology at our disposal, we still, to date, have not been able to perfect this fine art. The process is simple. All that is required is to practice the above steps in every facet of your life, and watch a dramatic change with the absolute minimum effort. Let this become a lifestyle-forming habit. It has been said that one of the greatest failures in achieving results through leadership is failure to communicate. Dissemination of information is an ongoing process and must be maintained with consistence for favorable results.

---

[50] Mitchell Costa – Intimacy in Marriage –Struikhof – Cape Town - 1991

Chapter 7

Paradigm Shift

A paradigm is our mental framework on a given topic or concern. It is our fundamental perspective, consisting of the guidelines, values, priorities, and sets of ideas we live by. These perspective patterns or models, are incredibly powerful. They determine outcomes.[51]

In the book of Genesis 1:26 – **Then God said, "let us make man in our own image, in our likeness, and let them rule over the fish of the sea and the birds of the air, over the live-stock, over all the earth and over all creatures that move along the ground."**

Essentially, what God was saying – let us craft and design an architectural reflection or representation of us – an image or likeness a structure that we may dwell in. Therefore, man, first and foremost, must reflect God. Second, he must have dominion. Third, he must have the ability to create. Hence, the capacity of his mind is unlimited. All of this took place in a spiritual world. As the result of the fall – Gen 2:15 – another world came into existence. Apart from the spiritual world, a natural world was born. At this juncture, the full capacity of the mind, ceased to exist. This limitation has affected the destiny of man.

What causes us to think like the way we do? How does a certain mind set establish itself and steer us from past generations, to present and future generations – controllable and uncontrollable?

Certain limitations have been placed on us that have become a way of life which we have accepted.

---

[51] Rinehart Stacy – Upside down – NavPress – Colorado – 1998

Some of the systems that have engraved our thinking and thought processes, patterns and lifestyles may be:

Colonialism

Many of the countries in Africa were colonialized by Western Powers. Hence, the culture of westernization became very prevalent. In South Africa, we were taught English and Afrikaans in schools – these were primarily the two official languages. Our mother tongue or cultural dialects would become a thing of the past. We were affected by certain laws of the state. Some of these laws were discriminatory laws, for example – the group areas act. This law separated us from living together in a mixed race community. We lived as a community within our race groups in geographical locations decided by the government. Certain areas were no-go areas, as it was against the law to go there, depending on the pigmentation of an individual's skin. Permission had to be obtained from authorities just to be able to drive through some areas.

The separate amenities act – this law prevented certain races from using facilities that were only for elite groups. We had to use facilities designated according to our race groups or classification. We had separate schools, transport systems, facilities, separate entrances and eating areas – even benches were marked with race classification. Service delivery, generally, was also according to race classifications with geographical locations.

The system of apartheid, a system of racial segregation enforced through legislation, was the rule of law we lived under. This system advocated a premise that certain race groups were superior to others. Certain benefits and privileges were based on the pigmentation, of your skin. This monopolized the entire economic system through job reservations, privileges etc. This resulted in an unequal society, the effects of which is still felt today in spite of the years of democracy.

Class System

The class or caste system was a type of xenophobia that separated us within our race groups. This mind-set, or system of thinking, was brought to South Africa by our fore fathers from India. The class or caste system, I am told, is still practiced but to a lesser extent. Many say that this was instigated by the colonialist or British Empire that ruled India at that time. This was a system used to divide and control. Some say that this was a practice of ancient times. Social status and association are determined by your class or caste. If you fall in the category of the Dalits or untouchables, you are looked down upon by society as being inferior. Any association with the untouchables is strictly forbidden. This was a divided system that caused irreparable damage to many generations. The primary criteria that qualified any marriage arrangement were decided by this system. Invitation to community and social functions were dictated to by this system.

Family history

Many of our lives were fashioned according to our family history. We were not only great believers, but also practitioners of tradition. Our living standards, education, employment, etc. was according to this tradition. In most cases, parents made sure that their children followed in their footsteps, especially in employment or business choices. Sometimes, this proved beneficial and other times, not a good choice.

In many cases, contribution to economic viability was determined by age and not education. The ability to provide for the family was more important than completion of schooling .Some parents were not able to provide their children with the means to further education because of financial constraints. There was a huge disparity between large families and income earned to support them. This placed limitations on children who had the potential and capabilities to peruse highly paid careers. Instead, many had to seek menial employment with low earnings. This gave rise to inferiority complexes. This placed barriers and limited breakthroughs in many families who could have progressed or advanced with raised levels of living. However, there were some that chose to explore and break limitations, is spite of limitations and constraints, resulting in great success. This success has been passed on to many generations. This has changed their destiny.

Mind-Sets or Self-Worth

There is rarely anything as powerful as a thought or idea. Our thoughts are products of what we have seen, learnt, heard or experienced. The origins of our thoughts determines the thoughts we conceive and who we eventually become. Our value systems and code of conduct is concluded by our thought process. Essentially, we are the sum total of our thoughts. Everything starts with a thought that becomes an idea. Ideas become ideologies. Ideologies conceived become beliefs. Beliefs conceived become convictions. Convictions conceived become philosophies. Philosophies conceived become lifestyles. Lifestyles determine our destinies.[52]

Self-worth or self-concept is a picture you have of yourself. Our self-image and self-concept are the first reality that must be established in our minds before we can effectively fulfil our purpose or destiny. A poor self-image or concept of ourselves will result a low evaluation of humanity. You cannot give significance if you don't already have it. Significance starts from within. Self-worth is not what others place on you but what you place on yourself.

These engravings on our minds have caused "pre-mature deaths." Many have, not only left this earth, but lived with unexplored potential and talents because of limitations placed upon us.

Vitezslav Gardavskv, the Czeck philosopher and martyr who died in 1978, said in his *book God Is Not Yet Dead,* the terrible threat against life, is not death, nor pain, nor any variation on the disasters that we so obsessively try to protect ourselves against with our social systems and personal stratagems. The terrible threat is "that we might die earlier than we really do die, before death has become a natural

---

[52] Munroe Myles – The Spirit of Leadership – USA - 2005

necessity. The real horror lies in just a "pre-mature death", a death after which we go on living for many years.[53]

These influences have affected us and have in some cases, reconfigured our entire generational psychological profile. Our paradigms or mental framework have been altered. In order to fully comprehend the whole concept of a paradigm shift, there has to be a change in our entire thought process. Our minds are programmed in a fashion which operates on a simple concept of "information intake is equal to behavior output." We behave according to the information or the knowledge we have. Hence, our knowledge of leadership is based on what we presume it to be. This can be based on learnt principles, experiences and examples set by others. To change the course of history will necessitate a paradigm shift. We need to start thinking beyond the capacity of our minds. Our old thinking patterns must become obsolete to some extent, and a new intake of information instituted. There is a deletion of some of the old and our thought patterns are now upgraded to a whole new philosophy and outlook of the concept of life. This has a direct ramification on leadership principles. There has to be a re-engineering of oneself.

Mind sets have to change and there has to be a migration to a different level of thought process. If we chose not to change, we will be dominated by appetite and impulse. Our lives will remain or become empty of commitment, purpose and continuity.

Basic foundational leadership issues have to be re-examined. Core values as shown in the bible and examples set by Jesus must be the platform from which to build structures. Unless this takes place, we will continue to fashion our values according to examples set and after

---

[53] Peterson H Eugene – Run With The Horses – Intervarsity Press-Downers Grove – 1983

influences of dominant characters or incidents that affect our lives during our learning and growing process.

Jeremiah 1:5 Reads:

Before I formed you in the womb of your mother I knew you, and before you were born I consecrated you; I appointed you a prophet to the nations.

Our destiny has been ordained before conception. Our life has been divinely designed before the foundation of the earth. Our inability to live out our true potential and purpose, because of limitations, is an indictment placed by us on ourselves.

My-self is given to me far more than it is formed by me. My-self is created in the image of God, after His likeness. I possess the ability to break limitations, do the impossible, scale walls that cause obstructions and achieve that which was declared according God's word. No matter what the situation is, we are more than over comers because of the Power of God that dwells in us. We are not defined by the colour of our skin, ethnicity, our social or economic status; we are defined by our identity – the children of the Most High God. It is not our feelings, or backgrounds that determine our level of participation in life, nor our experiences – good or bad – it's what God decides about us.

Our lives have to be shaped by visions that define destiny, not by fashions of the day and mind-sets or feelings about ourselves.

There is an enormous gap between what we think we can do, and what we really can do! Therefore, we dare to venture into what was feared to be forbidden territory or impossible. Then we become, the sum total of our belief system, which replaces fear with faith. We engage the full capacity of our thought process that dares us to break all kinds of limitation and realize break through that was never seen in the history of our forefathers. We are architects of blessed and prosperous future generations. We are chain breakers that bring about liberation that will effect generations, whom we may never live to see. We will leave behind a legacy that will re-write history.

Life is not an inevitable decline into dullness; for some it is an ascent into excellence.[54]

---

[54] Ibid

Chapter 8

The Challenge of Change

One day while driving down Great East Road, in Lusaka, Zambia, I noticed this statement painted on the wall of the Agricultural Show Grounds. This really got me thinking. I realised that if only the laziness or unwillingness to embrace change is eradicated, more than half of our problems would be resolved or simply just dissolve. I also began to recall some of my personal experiences and realised that, change is indeed, a challenge.

Change is one of the fundamental pillars of leadership. By virtue of its meaning, it is more often, an absolute challenge. Hence, *the challenge of change*.

Life is progressive, dynamic, changing and growing. One of the most significant resistances to change is the fear of failure. Fear of failure is common to man. But, the irony of this situation is that the inability to change is in itself failure.

Winston Churchill once said "there is nothing wrong with change, if it is in the right direction." The suggestion of change is not necessarily an indictment on our predecessors or that they may have lacked insight.

Positive change is good and a huge benefit to any organization. It brings about transformation, which seriously needs to take place. It also brings about new and innovative ideas that promote growth and development. John Walter, the president of AT&T said, "When the pace of change outside an organization becomes greater than the pace of change inside the organization, the end is near."

Myles Munroe, in his book, *Seasons of Change,* states:

Change is a component of time. Time produces change. Therefore, everything that is within time experiences change. Time is an interruption in eternity and a measure of forever. God created time, as required in the first book of Moses. Its purpose is clearly stated in the words… "to mark seasons and days and years" (Genesis 1:14). In essence, time was created to give eternity a measure manifested in season and years. The term "seasons" denote change. Therefore, the creation of time became the source of change.[55]

Myles Munroe makes a further observation:

"Every organization committed to impacting its environment must consider the prospect of change and its ability to respond effectively to that change. No organization exists in a vacuum. Each must submit to the demands of its environments, and the demands vary as the environment changes. Even the most passive organization is compelled in its environment. There are reluctant organizations in aggressive environments.

The message and purpose of the church is constant and unchanging, but its programs, methods, and mechanisms often lag behind the culture and become irrelevant. The challenge of the church in the 21st century is to adapt without adopting the values of surrounding culture. After all, a turn in the road is not the end of the road, unless you fail to make the turn.[56]

Max Ways, in *The Era of Radical Change*, stated:

Change has always been a part of the human condition. What is different now is the pace of change, and the prospect that it will come faster, effecting every part of life, including personal values, morality, and religion, which seem almost remote from technology… so swift

---

[55] Munroe Myles-Seasons of Change-Pneuma life Publishing-Lanham-1998
[56] Munroe Myles-Seasons of Change-Pneuma life Publishing-Lanham-1998

is the acceleration, that trying to "make sense" of change will become our basic industry.[57]

Change is inevitable. In life the only constant is change. Adapt or get left behind. Changing mind-sets is one of the most difficult tasks that have to be overcome by leadership. Generally, people, by nature, resist change. The simple reason being that people inadvertently, settle in a comfort zone. Change is seen as interference and upsets the stability of this comfort zone. When this stability is threatened, the challenges of changing mind-sets now turn into a battle. In most cases we hear more about why things cannot be done than why they can be. Therefore, with change come challenges.

The challenge of change, ultimately, has a two prong process. Firstly, in order to implement effectively, the leaders must understand the implication of change itself. Secondly, the process of change must be understood and "bought by" the affected group.

If all goes well, as above, then change is easily implemented.

Unfortunately, this is not always the case. Not all people, at all times, will accept change for various reasons. Herein, is the challenge.

Many great organizations that have once emerged as giants are no longer in existence. Yet, on the other hand, many once small organizations have now emerged as giants. It all boils down to the ability to change and stay relevant. One of the reasons for the success of these organizations was the ability not only to change, but to also overcome the challenges of change.

Even though people know that situations can never remain the same, or be as they would like them to be, they still continue to resist. The mere word *change* often produces an emotional reaction. Change brings challenge to those who lead. Because of these challenges, leaders need to understand the forces at work and the emotions that create resistance. Effective leaders, not content with passive

---

[57] Ways Max – The Era of Radical Change – Fortune - 1964

acceptance of their ideas, try to obtain support for any worthwhile changes.[58]

A wise person said, "People resist being changed, rather than resist change itself." In order to initiate change, leaders must identify existing resistance, diagnose it, and confront it with planned strategies.[59]

Reasons for resistance to change

Gordon L. Lippit in his book *Organizational Renewal* has scientifically analyzed some of the reasons people in organizations resist change.[60]

1. Purpose and nature of change not made clear

Purpose refers to why and what refers to the nature of the change. When this is not made clear, it causes uncertainty and in some cases anxiety. Fear of the unknown is more disruptive than the actual change itself. Even if change only affects a small number in a particular work group, everybody must be made aware of the change. People also oppose vague and general changes rather than specific ones.

To avoid this, the leader must –

- Warn people of any considered change.
- Communicate directly with the entire group likely to be effected by the change.

2. Lack of participation in the planning of change

People resent and resist when –

---

[58] D'Souza Anthony – Leadership – Paulines Publications - 2003
[59] Ibid
[60] Lippit L Gordon - Organisational Renewal – Appleton Century Cross- New York - 1969

- They are not involved in planning of change
- They find out afterwards

When people have a voice in the actual planning, they are more likely to accept and support what they helped to create.

3. Fear of failure and loss of status

The lack of mastering new skills, especially in the field of technology, causes people to fear. This also may have an impact on their status. If, for example, computer literacy is now needed – old fashioned thinkers feel threatened as a new breed of individuals seem to now be in control of things.

Leaders need to provide for training for existing people. This will ensure that people are given the opportunity to learn new skills that are required.

4. Fear of loss of self esteem

Pride and achievement builds self-esteem. Consciously or unconsciously, people have a strong fear of losing that self-esteem.

5. Break up of social groups

People have the tendency to work with selected groups. They fear that any changes may affect the stability of their various groups. In many instances, they have been together for a long period of time. A change may seem as interference.

Ultimately, change will happen, whether accepted or not. Therefore, implementation is important. Change cannot be held back because of people's inadequacies or fears of change. Change must be implemented in order to be current.[61]

---

[61] Lippit L Gordon - Organizational Renewal – Appleton Century Cross- New York - 1969

Jesus brought more change and profound newness to life than anyone else in the history of the world. As a result, he was challenged and met every challenge with beautifully thought-out responses

Enforcing change

As discussed, change is inevitable. It will and must happen in order to stay relevant at a particular time and age. The problem does not solely rely in the actual process of change, but also in the bringing about or enforcing change. This can have a positive or negative effect. It all depends on the execution of the process. Change, in its entirety, is or should be positive, not necessarily for an individual or group, but for the entire organization.

The marketing of this change to the various role players is of utmost importance. We need to understand that there will have to be change in mind-sets. This is not easy. Resistance to change should not be met with hostility, but with a challenge. Therefore, the enforcing of change must be done with creative minds that are able to predict any foreseeable ramifications.

If change is one way downward, this will lead to negative tension. People naturally resist if pressure is put on them. Often leaders are placed in unpopular situations, where change has to take place and is not bought by the various role players. When leaders facilitate change, resistance is immediately removed and change becomes acceptable. In initiating change, effective leaders help people express their feelings. Adjusting and accepting usually comes more easily when people share in the process.

Anthony D'Souza in his book – Developing the Leader within You – Strategies for Effective Leadership – gives us some practical suggestions for building a climate of mutual trust in the midst of change situations.[62]

---

[62] D'Souza Anthony – Developing the Leader Within You – Singapore - 1994

Explain why

Effective leaders provide all the facts and reasons for change. If it involves risks, he acknowledges that, and explains why the risks are worth taking and what they are doing to minimize that risk.

State the benefits of the change

Effective change leaders do not exaggerate. At the same time, not to state the benefits would be like a salesperson not telling a customer what the product can do.

Invite participation

Effective leaders of change request suggestions because the people involved know the situation best. Changes work out more favorably when those concerned participate in the change.

Seek questions and answer them

Wise leaders know that open communication stops rumors that inevitably arise during organizational change.

Avoid surprises

When leaders surprise workers with something they did not expect, they create unreasoning resistance. Emotions take over, and they are often strongly negative. They also lose trust in their leaders.

Acknowledge the rough spots

Presenting a clear-cut chart can make organizational shifts sound simple. Yet even a minor change is rarely simple. Effective change leaders admit difficulties and explain how the organization plans to smooth it out.

Set Targets

People need to know when the organization expects the changes to be completed. Leaders need to tell them what they expect under the new system and when they expect to have it operational. They also discuss the possibility of failure, and what it would mean, as well as the rewards for success.

Show appreciation and support

In any situation, people feel anxious. Leaders need to show appreciation and positively reinforce workers.

Contact informal leaders

Effective leaders have learned early that if they communicate with informal leaders, telling them what is going on, they have a better chance of success.

Dr. John N. ChaCha in his book, Ten Pillars of Christian Leadership, makes some interesting observations:[63]

The forefront of Christian leadership today is filled with leaders who have such a pioneering mentality.

- They display a self-reliant and self-motivated spirit.
- They are alert to new opportunities, active and eager to explore new heights.
- They are opportunity-hunters who display ingenuity in anticipating and meeting unexpected situations.
- They are God seekers.
- They exhibit a cool head.
- They have the ability to objectively process ideas and evaluate how those ideas will impact their goals.
- They are decisive in their choices.
- They enjoy turning adverse situations to work for their advantage.

---

[63] ChaCha John – 10 Pillars of Leadership – Teamwork study Publication.

- They are not afraid of the unexpected.
- They welcome change because it creates opportunities.

These attributes mentioned by Dr. ChaCha are excellent for leadership and change development. Unfortunately, this only exists in an ideal world - we do not live in an ideal world. Therefore, I think the appropriate word to include in the above statements is *suppose* after the word *they*.

Dr. ChaCha makes further interesting observations:[64]

Good changes bring growth and new life into an organization. A leader must use his influence to re-structure faulty organizations. There can never be growth without changes. In fact, change is an indispensable pillar for building successful leadership.

Sometimes we have to experience pain, or even some sacrifices, before we can make lasting changes. When a leader is unwilling to make necessary changes or sacrifices in any aspect of life, he soon becomes obsolete in his leadership. He becomes a stumbling block to the organization. His usefulness as a leader becomes limited.

A leader must be flexible enough to adapt or change his methods to fit the circumstances, even if he has a wide range of resources. Flexibility to change or adapting is necessary for growth and improvement.

Hebrews 7:11-12 gives us an example of a biblical adaption:

"If perfection could have been attained through the Levitical priesthood (for on the basis of it the law was given to the people), why was there still need for another priest to come – one in the order of Melchizedek, not in the order of Aaron? For when there

---

[64] ChaCha John – 10 Pillars of Leadership – Teamwork study Publication.

is a change of the priesthood, there must also be a change of the law."

Another great example of a change in leadership is found in the book of Joshua. Israel was a new nation. Moses was the leader whom the people related to. When it came time for a change of leadership from Moses to Joshua, the environment had changed dramatically. Many believe that by this time of transition, Joshua was an expert in dealing with issues in the wondering mode. Suddenly there is a reality check. It was time to enter the promised land and conquer those that occupied it. Moses, by this time, had reached the end of his era. He was preparing to meet his eternal destiny. Joshua seems uncertain. Hence, God spoke to him.

Joshua 1:9 reads:

"Have I not commanded you? Be strong and courageous! Do not tremble and be dismayed, for the Lord your God is with you wherever you go."

There is only one explanation as to why God told Joshua not to be afraid – he was afraid. Change was being born. There was a changing of the guard. Joshua almost panicked. However, he took God's word – when God said "Go" he followed instructions and in verse 10 and 11, he took responsibility

Criticism is an inevitable aspect of change. With change comes progress and new direction. If, for any reason, this is not evident, leaders become the visible target. This is, in spite of change being progressive. Most times, evidence of change takes a period of time to manifest before any effects are evident. Leaders still have to face the brunt of disgruntled followers. Warranted or not, leaders cannot prevent the venting of feelings. This should not prevent them from continuing to make decisions, popular or unpopular. The course, vision or mandate of the organization cannot be altered in response to popular opinion. Wise leaders always surround themselves with people who are able to challenge ideas, offer alternate options and engage in constructive dialogue. Leaders should accept legitimate contributions which emanate out of constructive engagement. This by no means advocates a democracy, but a Theocracy must be the end result.

Destructive criticism must be addressed and underlying motivation exposed. Leaders should not feel threatened or take responses personally and no longer make decisions that are necessary. Loyal opposition is healthy and must be viewed as such.

J. Oswald Sanders, a former leader of the China Mission, comments, "Often the crowd does not recognize a leader until he has gone, and then they build a monument for him with the stones they threw at him in life."[65]

However, rejection is sometimes deserved when changes are implemented to suit personal agendas, unreasonable demands and lack of credibility. Jesus experienced enormous popularity and undeserved rejection: "Even in His own land and among His own people, He was not accepted." (John 1:11)

Change is Inevitable –With or without criticism- Adapt or Die. Meaning, we will become irrelevant and will soon be extinct. Change is a choice. If we chose to change we will be relevant and our ability to exist in months and years to come will be successful. Either way – there are consequences.

In the words of Mahatma Gandhi "Be the change you wish to see in the world." Imagine the consequences if we heeded this.

---

[65] Quoted by Gibbs, Eddie – Leadership Next – Intervarsity Press – UK – 2005.

Chapter 9

Stress Management

Stress is an age old condition that has never been managed or overcome to any extreme. We read about it, know about it, and experience it in almost every facet of our lives. Almost seventy percent of the stress that we contend with is not consciously perceived, but still causes damage. This has become one of the leading causes or aggravation of physical ailments, some with detrimental effects, which are suffered by many in our day and age.

This condition dates back to the beginning of time and has seen its fair course through the pages of history. Many biblical characters, both in the Old Testament and New Testament, including Jesus, suffered a fair amount of stress. This verifies the fact that none of us are exempt from this condition. Some may argue that the levels of stress we experience today are a direct result of some of the conditions that we are faced with. Meaning, we live in an environment which exhibits stress, and, therefore, this has become a way of life.

No matter what we do, or how we do it, stress seems to surface as a common denominator. This is true within certain parameters. Stress is here to stay and this condition has become a way of life; we cannot sit back and accept this phenomenon as a norm. Unless we do something to manage this condition, we will not live life to its full potential. We will not enjoy life, nor the fruits of our efforts, as our existence will be short-lived.

The answer to the management of this condition is very clearly given to us in the book of Exodus chapter 18, when Jethro, Moses father-in-law, visited him. Let us further analyze this situation.

Exodus 18:13 reads:

"On the morrow Moses sat to judge the people and the people stood about Moses from morning till evening."

Moses set up an office (so to speak) to consult with the people regarding their problems. He was the only counselor consultant and, therefore, worked from morning till evening. It does not appear that he had finished in the evening. He concluded only because the day had come to an end. He continued on the morning of the next day.

Verse 14 reads:

When Moses father-in- law saw all that he was doing for the people he said, "what is this you are doing for the people? Why do you sit alone, and all the people stand about you from morning till evening?"

In verse 15 and 16, Moses goes on to explain his management by crisis actions.

Verse 17 reads:

Moses' father-in-law said to him, "what you are doing is not good. You and the people will wear yourselves out, for the thing is too heavy for you. You are not able to perform it alone."

Moses was doing *right wrongly* – sounds like a paradox, but true. In essence, what Jethro was telling Moses is that he (Moses) was taking on more than he could handle. Jethro's words were, "for the thing is too heavy for you." His capacity to manage the situation had been exhausted long before the day was out. Simply meaning, Moses was being stressed out through poor leadership practices.

The irony of this situation is that Moses was doing well by trying to resolve the issues of the people. He tried to govern with order, ensuring there were no unresolved issues and that as far as possible, everybody was happy. Yet Jethro tells him that what he (Moses) was doing was not good. Jethro was referring to the self-infliction of stress that Moses was bringing upon himself.

There was no point in Moses trying to resolve issues of the people at the detriment of his own health. Moses was the leader of the children of Israel. Therefore, his ability to lead, and the requirement to be on guard was of utmost important. In order for him to function effectively, his faculties must not be impaired. What good will he be as a leader, if he was unable to function effectively as one? If he continued to function as he did, how much could he give off in the short term? His leadership abilities would have definitely been impaired. He would soon be of absolutely minimum or no use at all. Meaning that, he would not have been able to bring to conclusion what God had intended for him to do.

In verse 19 – Jethro gives Moses wise counsel.

Verse 19 to 22 reads:

"Listen now to my voice; I will give thee counsel, and God be with you. You shall represent the people before God, and you shall teach them the statutes and the decisions, and make them know the way in which they must walk and what they must do. Moreover, choose able men from all the people, such as fear God, men who are trustworthy and who hate a bribe; and place such men over the people as rulers of thousands, of hundreds, of fifties, and of tens. And let them judge the people at all times; every great matter they shall bring, but any small matter they shall decide themselves; so it will be easier for you, and they will bear the burden with you."

In these verses Jethro gives Moses excellent advice on the principles of management – Planning, Leading, Controlling, Leading and Delegation. He also gives Moses the formula for effective leadership.

Here is a summary of the important lessons:

- Teach them the statutes – rules or laws.

Ensure that the people are informed, taught and are aware of the rules of the game or the key drivers that govern them. If they are aware, much of the issues will be resolved among themselves. They will become mature and will have the ability to handle first line grievances. Impartation or transfer of knowledge through the medium of teaching will also enhance their ability and confidence to eradicate trivial or unimportant issues. Here the need for training and development as discussed in previous chapters are very evident.

- Choose able men from among the people – God fearing, trustworthy, morally upright with unquestionable integrity.

Choose men who will meet the qualifications for leadership. This is necessary for effective results. People need to know that these men have principles and have the ability to assist with issues, preferably, with knowledge and experience. People need to have confidence that these men can be trusted to resolve issues with the utmost integrity and honesty.

These are excellent qualities of choice for leadership. Moses had to ensure that the initial formulas that form foundational principles of leadership are not compromised. Note that Jethro did not ask Moses to choose men he liked, or men of status, financially viable or family members etc. Jethro was specific on conditions of choice. However, it cannot be discounted that these people may also have the qualities that Jethro advised to select. But note the priority qualifications – all else is secondary.

- Place them as rulers of thousands, hundreds, fifties and tens.

Jethro asked Moses to form leadership organizational structures based on relational models. This is evident by the call for leaders to interact with groups and resolve issues, particularly, of conflict. There are different levels of leadership based on capabilities to lead in accordance to specific strengths. He also wanted a leadership protocol or line function leadership. He specifically gave instructions to divide groups in numbers for easy administrative purposes. This also allows for easy control and streamlining protocols for effective results.

Five leaders of ten will report to leaders of fifties. Two leaders with fifty under their control will report to leaders of a hundred. Ten leaders of a hundred will report to leaders of a thousand. There will be several structures put in place consisting of these segments.

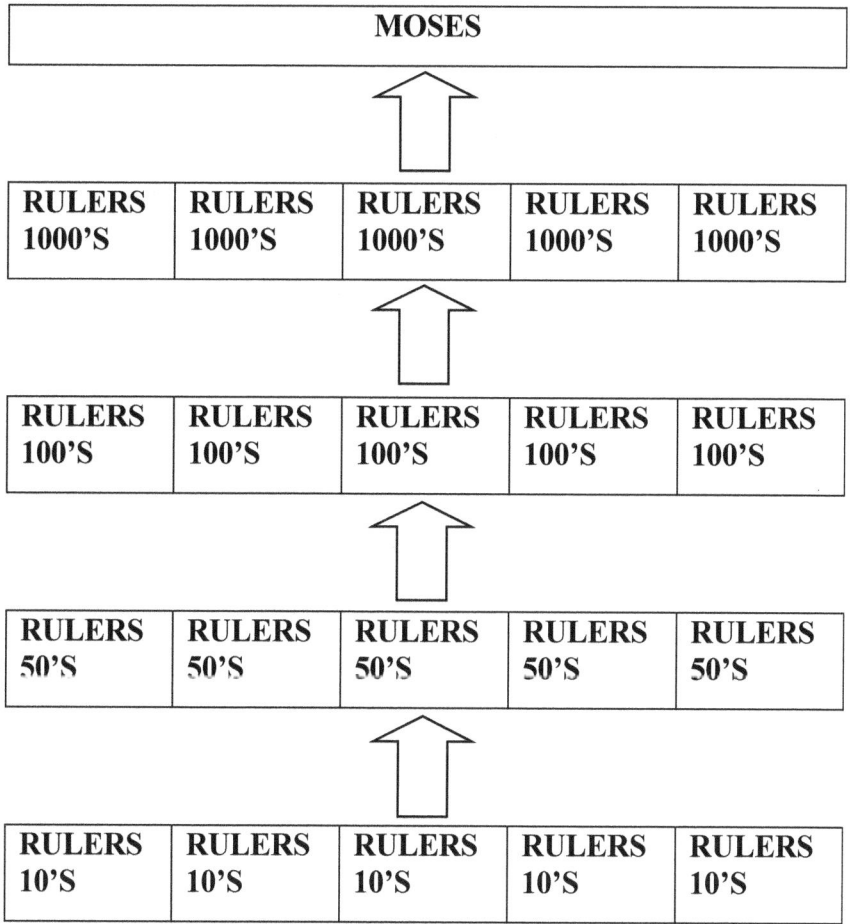

- Every great matter – they must bring to you – all small matters must be resolved by themselves.

Moses will lead or manage by exception. Line leaders must be mandated to resolve issues of less importance. Issues of importance must be resolved along the leadership line function. Any unresolved issues of importance will be referred to Moses. Moses now has specific issues to deal with. These issues will require expertise that he possesses and will be resolved with the absolute minimum stress.

In addition to the creation of the organizational structure, the origins of the principles of leadership and management are very evident. These principles, as mentioned above are planning, leading, organizing, controlling and delegation. In addition to this, conflict resolution was managed and solved with absolute minimum of inconvenience. Through experience, we all know that if a problem or conflict is unresolved at base or grass root level, it compounds itself, with complications as it escalates to higher levels.

Jethro saw that Moses was extremely stressed – he wanted to help Moses to alleviate his stress by giving him proper advice. In a nutshell, a decentralised form of administration was implemented. This resulted in shared responsibility. Ultimately, performances are upgraded if we capitalize on our strengths and delegate our weaknesses.

Again, the irony of this exercise is that **Moses was doing right wrong**. We read and know this story, but I think now we see it in a different light.

Let us look at some scientific information regarding stress.

Stress can be defined as nervous tension that results from internal conflicts from a wide range of external situations.

I found out, much to my amazement, that stress is not pressure that is experienced from external factors. Stress is primarily caused by our reaction to these factors. Stress begins with being anxious, which leads to anxiety, which leads to tension. Tension, from the word tense, creates a type of panic behavior. The result of this panic behavior is very evident when a person becomes "touchy." This reaction is because of our mental and psychological profiles being affected, due to being anxious. A person's entire profile is altered due to strain on the mental and psychological framework. These can have altering capabilities that changes behavior patterns, social stability and relational attributes. When a person gets to this point, whether noticeable or not, it clearly confirms that stress is the major factor.

Stress also stems out of conflict situations. Our withholding capacity is sometimes tested to limits which are beyond what we are able to handle. This causes chaos in our mind, it seems like excessive pressure to which we are unable to respond. Our thought process lacks the ability to make on-time emotional adjustments.

However, not all stress is bad. There is also another aspect of stress which has positive contributions. This is called eustress or positive stress. This type of stress increases performance and acts as a type of motivator to achieve goals and deadlines. It increases and challenges the quest for achievement.

Hans Selye, one of the world's leading experts on stress clearly defines stress based on scientific research:[66]

What stress is not

Stress isn't the influence of a negative occurrence. Stress isn't an entirely bad event.

What stress is

Stress is the mobilization of the body's defenses that allow human beings to adapt to hostile or threatening events. Stress is a state manifested by a specific syndrome of biological events that can be both pleasant and unpleasant.

Stress is dangerous when unduly prolonged, comes too often, or concentrates on one particular organ of the body.

Stress has three faces:

1. **Distress** is the negative feature. People normally associate stress with anxiety, tension, strain, pain, and frustration. It

---

[66] Hans Selye – The Stress of Life – New York – McGraw Hill - 1976

comes from pressure situations, uptight feelings, and unpleasant encounters, personal and professional demands.

2. **Eustress**, the positive form, appears when people face an exciting challenge.

3. **Neutral** evokes negative feelings at first, but if properly handled, can turn to positive experiences. For example, conflict reminds of unpleasant encounters with people. Yet, such encounters can result in positive experiences of clearing the air.

THE THREE ASPECTS OF STRESS[67]

DISTRESS (Negative stress)	STRESS (Neutral stress)	EUSTRESS (Positive stress)
Anxiety	Conflict	Challenge
Tension	Crisis	Opportunity
Strain	Change	Achievement
Worry	Deadlines	Creativity
Fear	Schedules	Promotion
Annoyance	Criticism	Progress
Exasperation	Expectations	Success
Anger	People	Affection
Hate	Communication	Friendship
Confusion	Issues	Love
Frustration	Problems	Marriage
Misunderstanding		Sex
Discontent		Family
Pain		Vacation
Disappointment		Excitement
Fatigue		Stimulation
Insomnia		

---

[67] Hans Selye – The Stress of Life – New York – McGraw Hill - 1976

Causes of Stress

The cause of stress varies from person to person. This depends on the ability that a person has, based on tolerance levels. To some people an incident, however serious it may be, has no bearing on them. However, to others, the same incident may have repercussions that may be beyond their ability to handle. This will stress them out. People often have the tendency to blame external forces rather than to look within themselves. Almost 90% of the stress we experience is self-imposed through our behavior, beliefs and sometimes our personalities. The fear or the consequences of what might happen can cause stress. Anthony D'Souza outlines some of the causes.[68]

- Trying to control or change things over which we have no control.

Some people spend a lot of time thinking about mistakes they can't change or wishing other people would be different.

- Fighting changes that must come about.

Some people cannot let go of old methods that have become obsolete.

- Worrying about the future.

As productive and effective as planning is, when people get overly concerned about all the things that could happen, it is not conducive to health and well-being. More attention or focus must be on the present.

- Unrealistic high goals and self-blame.

Although people want to achieve, they need to realize that they cannot fully meet every demand.

---

[68] D'Souza Anthony – Leadership – Paulines Publications - 2003

Anxiety

Generally, the absence of joy ultimately leads to anxiety. This is caused as a result of several things. Often it is the inability to meet the requirements of any particular task. It can also stem from fear of several things: failure, loss of popularity, confrontation, opposition, dealing with people etc. Fear of success can also result in anxiety.

One of the subtle causes, especially in leadership is loneliness. The irony of this phenomenon is, in spite of being surrounded by people, the element of psychological loneliness seems to play a huge part in the lives of leaders. It is the loneliness of having to make decisions that affects the lives of people. It is the loneliness of a leader that carries the burden to lead with passion and conviction. It is the loneliness that becomes a reality when leaders are deserted by their followers. Most painful is the absence of friends and close associates.

In Psalm 3: 7, 10, 11-13, 17, 22 – David cries to God with anguish in the midst of painful experiences. He sought the protection of the Lord, not only from his enemies, but also from his friends.

Jesus experienced extreme isolation in the Garden of Gethsemane. While He prayed, in anguish, His disciples slept (Mark 14:32-42).

The Apostle Paul suffered loneliness and abandonment in Asia. He reminded Timothy in 2 Timothy 1:15 – You know that everyone in the province of Asia has deserted me, including Phygelus and Hermogenes.

Some leaders experience loneliness out of self-infliction. Some prefer not to get to close to their subjects. They believe that there has to be a rank and file type of hierarchy – meaning that they are of a higher level. To get close will be a sign of weakness.

Eddie Gibbs makes an interesting comment, "Saints don't keep people at a distance; celebrities do."

Over and above being in leadership, many people work in increasingly demanding environments. The art of balancing work, church and family responsibilities can become extremely stressful. This type of stress cannot be avoided, but must be managed.

Signs of Stress

Certain indicators will prevail from time to time. These indicators may not be noticed or accepted by the affected person. However, it becomes very noticeable by others who are closely associated with them, especially, close friends and families. To deny these changes in behavior and in some cases, lifestyles, may have disastrous consequences.

Stress will reflect in symptoms that affects us in three profiles.[69]

1. **Psychological** - Worry or apprehension. Feelings of anxiety. Tenseness, sadness, agitation. Low self-esteem, feelings of rejection, depression. Feelings of failure. Irritability, tendency to lose temper, boredom, feelings of self-destruction.

2. **Behavioral** - Indecision or inability to make decisions. Inability to think clearly. Poor concentration. Inability to relax physically. Impulsive behavior, incompatible with normal pattern of behavior. Lack of desire to participate fully in life.

3. **Physiological Symptoms** – Muscle tension to spasms. Hypertension. Coronary heart disease, Ulcers, Skin rashes. Dizziness or blurred vision. Excessive tiredness. Chronic back pain. Insomnia. Chest pains or palpitations. Headaches. Shortness of breath.

When the body and mind are not in harmony, there is a conflict. This conflict must be brought under subjection. If the body and mind are still incompatible, stress will prevail.

Psychologists or Psychiatrists call this type of ailment psychosomatic illness. This is derived from the Greek word psyche, meaning "mind"

---

[69] Ibid

and soma, meaning "body". This illness results from the mind's influence over the body. This occurs when, instead of harmony between the mind and body, the mind seems to have a greater influence. This influence will affect the body negatively. Therefore, stress can play a major role in physical disease, which affects our bodies.

Coping with Stress

Leaders carry a great weight of responsibility. Apart from their internal influences, they have to deal with external issues. They are responsible for a number of accountabilities. There has to be total harmony in the different roles they play in their family life, vocational life, secular life and spiritual life. This can be extremely stressful. To obtain a balance, or maintain some sort of equilibrium is extremely difficult. Any additional time spent in any one of these roles, has to come from another role. This is an extremely tough balancing act to maintain.

The bible relates to many characters that have experienced intense stress. The Apostle Paul is one of them. In a study of 1 and 2 Corinthians the Apostle Paul relates some of his experiences and also the principles that carried him through.

1 Corinthians 2:3 reads:

"And I was with you in weakness and in much fear and trembling."

Corinth was a city that had a reputation of loose and violent living. He was emotionally stressed out. He arrived there with fear of the uncertainty, but was assured in God's word:

Verse 4"my speech and my message were not in plausible words of wisdom, but in demonstration of the Spirit and power,

Verse 5…that your faith might not rest in the wisdom of men but in the power of God."

This was the model Paul used as a survival strategy.

Jesus did, however, caution His disciples that those who decide to follow Him must take up the cross daily – Luke 9:23. Meaning that carrying the cross constituted a burden to shoulder.

2 Corinthians 1:8-11 reads:

"We do not want you to be uninformed brothers, about the hardships we suffered in the province of Asia. We were under great pressure, far beyond our ability to endure, so that we despaired even in life. Indeed, in our hearts we felt the sentence of death. But this happened that we might not rely on ourselves, but on God who raised the dead. He has delivered us from such a deadly peril, and He will deliver us. On Him we have set our hope that He will continue to deliver us, as you help us by your prayers."

Paul makes some startling statements that, no doubt, tell us of the enormous pressure he was under. Statements like "We were under great pressure, far beyond our ability to endure" and "Indeed in our hearts we felt the sentence of death," brings true definition to the word stress. Paul realizes his limitations and his human ability to cope with pressures that were far beyond his capacity to manage. He clearly says, "that we may not rely on ourselves, but on God who raises the dead. He has delivered us from such a deadly peril, and He will deliver us." Our strength, no matter who we are, has an exhaustive capability. Meaning, we will run out of steam, based on the energy of our own strength. Paul's affirmation of his anchor proves to be the ultimate reliability. So then, if Paul was stressed, means that we being stressed also is not an indictment on our character. It just reaffirms that we are human, and that we will be prone to the condition of stress.

However, the ability to cope with stress and not stress in its entirety, is the deciding factor. Like many other challenges in life, we can either overcome it or be subdued by it. It simply comes down to the ability to manage it.

Tom Marshall, in his *book Understanding Leadership*, highlights some great principals on biblical stress management.[70]

It is in the extremities of our strength that we run into God's strength.

Our capacity has limits. These limits may vary from person to person, but, it exists within us. God's strength is inexhaustible. It is our ability to tap into this inexhaustible source, in order to find solace. If we continue to tread on the limits of our reserves, with no divine source to draw from, we will eventually burn out. It is also at this point, we are able to recognize the divine provision. The Apostle Paul made it very clear when he said "He has delivered us from such a deadly peril, and He will deliver us. On Him we have set our hope the He will continue to deliver us." Meaning, God has delivered us, is delivering us, and will continue to deliver us.

Past deliverance gives secure grounds for future hope.

In bad times we need to remember the good times. This emphasizes the importance of recall. We remember our past experiences of God's faithfulness and mercy. There is always a bigger picture. We cannot look at any particular incident in isolation. We need to look at our experiences in the grand scheme of things. We have the benefit of divine intervention through prayer. All that is required from us is the ability to trust in this divine resource.

Lamentations 3:21-23 reads:

"Yet this I call to mind and therefore I have hope – because of the Lord's great love we are not consumed, for his compassions never fail. They are new every morning; great is Thy faithfulness."

At the point of recall, we remember what the Lord has done for u, and we discover that His mercies are forever and ever. They are new every morning, new every morning – great is Thy faithfulness.

---

[70] Marshall Tom – Understanding Leadership –Clays Limited- England-1991

In our need, we turn toward the body for its prayers.

We have not been called as leaders to operate like hermits in solitary confinement. Neither are we immune nor superior to everyday influences and challenges, both negative and positive. We need to be upheld in prayer more, purely, on the basis of our responsibilities. We need to have the ability to keep going, even though others are giving up. Independence can lead to self-sufficiency. Paul operated on the premise that he prayed for his people, he told them that he was praying for them, more than that, he asked them to pray for him. There is always a reservoir of concerned people that will always stand in the gap and intercede for leaders on a continual basis.

God always sets limits to what happens to us.

2 Corinthians 4:7 reads:

"But we have this treasure in jars of clay to show that this all surpassing power is from God and not from us. We are hard pressed on every side but not crushed; perplexed but not in despair; persecuted but not abandoned; struck down but not destroyed. We always carry around in our body the death of Jesus, so that the life of Jesus may also be revealed in our body."

Of particular note is "we are hard pressed on every side but not crushed; perplexed but not in despair; persecuted but not abandoned; struck down but not destroyed." Meaning, in spite of the odds against us, there is a sense of Godly preservation that seems to ultimately prevail. We will overcome, simply, because God always sets limits to what happens to us. When we embrace God's sovereign will in our lives, all of these circumstances come under His providence. We can rely on the sovereign providence which sets limits to what we are able to manage.

Remember the steadying influence of a divine perspective.

2 Corinthians 4:16-18 reads:

> "Therefore we do not lose heart. Though outwardly we are wasting away, yet inwardly we are being renewed day by day. For our light and momentary troubles are achieving for us an eternal glory that far outweigh them all. So we fix our eyes, not on what is seen, but what is unseen. For what is seen is temporary, but what is unseen is eternal."

From these verses of scriptures, it is very clear that Paul's perspective was not on the physical but on the eternal. Paul's standard of measurement was based on an eternal perspective. He also makes it very clear for us that our view should also be an eternal one. The physical perspective will bring stress and anxiety; the eternal perspective will bring joy and peace.

We are often governed by our perceptions. This also governs our emotions. When we perceive that we are in danger, fear sets in. When we perceive something is humorous we laugh. When we perceive that a greater resource is prevalent we tend to be more relaxed. Perception, ultimately defines reality.

Suffering is an inescapable part of growth.

2 Corinthians 6:3-10 reads:

> "We put no stumbling block in anyone's path, so that our ministry will not be discredited. Rather, as servants of God, we commend ourselves in every way; in great endurance, in troubles, hardships and distresses, in beatings, imprisonments and riots; in hard work, sleepless nights, and hunger; in purity, understanding, patience, and kindness; in the Holy Spirit, and in sincere love, in truthful speech and in the power of God; with weapons of righteousness in the right hand and in the left; through glory and dishonor, bad report and good report; genuine yet regarded as imposters; known yet regarded as unknown; dying and yet making many rich; having nothing and yet possessing everything."

Having read this scripture, it is very evident that what we sometimes consider hardships and stress amounts to almost nothing compared to what the apostle Paul experienced. The startling aspect about his statements is that, in spite of being highly stressed, he still offers encouragement. He realized that in all of his sufferings, the end result was that he was going to emerge victorious through Jesus Christ. Herein, lays our ability to realize that in all of our sufferings, there is growth and maturity. Hence, suffering is an inescapable part of growth.

As stated earlier, stress is an age old condition that has persisted and will continue to persist. We live in a post-modernist society.

Stress has become a way of life. Normal life is defined as stress being an ingredient. If this is not so, then our life appears to be boring, less challenging or "something is missing." In some instances, unless our adrenalin levels are high, we suffer with boredom.

Paul, apart from sharing his experiences, he also warned Timothy to be aware of this condition.

11 Timothy 3:1-5 reads:

"But understand this, that in the last days there will come times of stress. For men will be lovers of self, lovers of money, proud, arrogant, abusive, disobedient to their parents, ungrateful, unholy, inhuman, implacable, slanderers, profligates, fierce, haters of good, treacherous, reckless, swollen with conceit, lovers of pleasure than lovers of God, holding on to a form of religion but denying the power of it. Avoid such people."

This sounds like or rather, is a prophetic declaration. Paul just about covers everything that we are faced with in our daily lives. Even though this was written many centuries ago, we can confirm that everything Paul warns Timothy about is prevalent today.

Of significant note, take heed of the advice Paul gave Timothy. In closing, I consider Paul to be a man who possessed a high intensity of grace. It was this outrageous grace that gave him the ability to persist.

2 Corinthians 9:8 reads:

"And God is able to make all grace abound in you, so that in all things at all times, having all that you need, you will abound in every good work."

As John Maxwell said, "You are most valuable where you add the most value." This is ironic, yet accurate. Being stressed out adds no value.

Always remember, there are many things you can do, but, narrow this down to the things you must do. Being busy does not necessarily mean being productive.

Nobody is indispensable. Signs of being overwhelmed calls for drastic action. Leaders need to recognize the moments when limitations are becoming exhausted. Any attempts to continue under extreme stress will be self-destructive. The ultimate conclusion will be failure. Any decision not to continue is not an indictment on your character, potential and capacity, but a wise decision.

Often times, the presence of supportive people make a huge difference, especially when leaders get weary and discouraged with the load of leadership. These must be people who, even though they are a mix of temperament, must have a positive outlook.

It takes longer to recover from emotional exhaustion, than it does from physical exhaustion or sometimes rehabilitation from sickness. Emotional exhaustion requires "nurse type care" for full recovery.

Leaders must establish adequate safeguards to prevent themselves from demands placed on them. This includes the demands we place on ourselves, sometimes on a false sense of indispensability. Irrespective of who we are, we have limitations.

In Romans 12:12 – we are encouraged to be "joyful in hope, patient in affliction, faithful in prayer."

Chapter 10

Powerbased Leadership

Whenever a group of people are put to work together through any organisation, be it a company or a church, there must be some sort of a process, consisting of rules, procedures and policies or maybe a constitution. This forms the policy guidelines within which parameters are clearly defined. All concerned have to accept these controls, the extent and the limitations of power and the reciprocal conferring of authority with the acceptance of responsibility. The unfortunate situation is that theories of governance often conflict with personal agendas. What was originally designed for peace and harmony denigrates into lust for power. This results in insecurity within the organization, which has other repercussions, poor estimation of their work, lack of confidence etc. If left unattended, power structures begin to emerge.

There is an arguable controversy when a contrast is made between leadership in the world and leadership in the Kingdom. Leadership in the world practices from a platform of power and authority. Often times, the world leads through manipulation, personal charisma, or subtle intimidation. This is also often practiced in many churches. The misuse of power seems to flourish in many churches. Here human ambition is coated with a veneer of spirituality. This concept of power leadership has crept into our organizations and is working against every principle that the bible talks about. Leadership is about connection not controlling. Many are obsessed with their calling, genuine or not. All others are marginalized to serve.

God's calling applies to the totality of God's people. It is not restricted to leaders. This is an important point, not just for followers to grasp, but for leaders themselves who have a strong sense of calling. The myth of the 'restricted call' has crippled the mission in the world. Traditionally, the 'highest calling' has been labelled as 'full time service'. This has created two distinct classes of Christians – the clergy, those who are ordained to the pastorate, and the laity, the majority from which the few are selected.[71]

Clergy means called (*kletos*). This has an unspoken implication that the laity in not chosen or called by God. Subsequently, the church is built around the call and gifting of this elite group surrounded by a marginalized laity. This separation, on one hand, breeds resentment and struggles for power and influence; however, on the other hand, passivity and the avoidance of responsibility over spiritual matters, issues that are regarded as the domain of the clergy.[72]

The term laity (*laos*) has to be restored to its original meaning. – the people of God called to a priestly and apostolic ministry. (2 Corinthians 6:16; Titus 2:14; 1 Peter 2:9).[73] If this principle is embraced, the entire outlook of ministry responsibilities is seen is a different light. This becomes the basis which sees the demise of power structures and particularly, the loner types, autocratic, central power based church and organizations.

Eddie Gibbs quotes James Emery White from his book Embracing the Mysterious God.

"When personal fulfilment is allowed to take the place of calling, our lives become little more than exercises in self-indulgence. Ironically, we were created such that our deepest fulfilment is found as we submit to God's calling on our life. The reason is simple; we are first and foremost to someone, not to something or to somewhere.[74]

The religious system that developed in Israel after the Babylonian captivity had become the only means through which the people of Israel were taught to reach God. This placed enormous power in the

---

[71] Gibbs Eddie – Leadership Next – Intervarsity Press – UK - 2005
[72] Ibid
[73] Ibid
[74] Gibbs Eddie – Leadership next – Inter varsity press – UK 2005

hands of a few men. Like the Sanhedrin, much of the leadership today believe and do in the realm of power, authority and control. Historically, institutional authority has been confused with spiritual authority.[75]

Henri Nouwen in his book *Reflections on Christian Leadership* states:

One of the greatest ironies of the history of Christianity is that its leaders constantly gave in to the temptation of power –political power, military power, economic power, moral power, and spiritual power – even though they continued to speak in the Name of Jesus, who did not cling to his divine power but emptied Himself and became as we are.[76]

The reality is that there is an epidemic of power leadership loose in our churches and ministry organizations. Power leadership is so common that we have lost our immunity to this style of leadership. Decisions are made for people rather than with people. Doing is deemed more important in our ministries than being.[77]

Followers have become tools that leaders use to accomplish ends. People are of worth to the leader as long as they participate dutifully without questioning any decisions or authority. Any deviation from the mandate of the leader is seen as revolt or sedition and is branded by using the example of Moses and Korah. This is undeniably seen as total rebellion against the church even though the disagreement or difference in opinion was based on policy and ethics not doctrine.

Alister McGrath in his book – *Power Religions* explains:

There are remarkable, and disturbing, parallels between the distorted idea of priesthood in the medieval churches and the notion of ministry found within modern power evangelism. Both are intensely authoritarian. Both rest upon the ideology of power, which places the

---

[75] Rinehart Stacy – Upside down – NavPress – Colorado – 1998
[76] Nouwen Henri – Reflections on Christian Leadership – New York - 1989
[77] Rinehart Stacy – Upside down – NavPress – Colorado – 1998

right to speak for God in the hands of small and unaccountable elite. Both studiously ignore the possibility that they might get God wrong, and the deeply threatening and humiliating possibility that God might choose to challenge and correct them through ordinary lay folk within their undervalued congregations.[78]

The Old Testament records a phenomenal example of a king called Rehoboam, the son of Solomon. Solomon always surrounded himself with wise counsellors. It was hoped that this culture would be passed on to Rehoboam, and to future generations as a recipe for successful ruler ship of Israel.

Following the death of Solomon, Rehoboam was crowned the King of Israel. Before the coronation, the people appointed Jeroboam to represent them as liaison to the king.

1 Kings 12:4 reads:

"Your father made our yoke hard; now therefore lighten the hard service of your father and his heavy yoke which he put on us, and we will serve you."

In the latter years of Solomon's rule, he became very ambitious with making Israel an epicentre of culture. He achieved this through aggressive building campaigns. The citizens of Israel bore the brunt of this venture. It was during these latter days Rehoboam strayed from the Solomon's culture of wise counsel. The taxes were high and they were forced to allocate an unrealistic amount of time to construction work. They were practically reduced from citizen status to slaves. So, realistically speaking, when Solomon died, people wanted a break. They pledged their support to Rehoboam, in the hope that he would lead them differently from his father.

Here is Rehoboam's initial response:

1 Kings 12:5, 6 reads:

---

[78] McGrath Alister – Power Religion – Moody – Chicago - 1992

Then he said to them, "Depart for three days, then return to me." So the people departed. King Rehoboam consulted with the elders who had served his father Solomon while he was still alive, saying, "How do you counsel me to answer this people?"

So far, so good. This is a mark of a great leader – seeking advice and listening to wise counsel because his father's advisors were well positioned to guide him.

Here is their response:

1 Kings 12:7 reads:

Then they spoke to him, saying "If you will be a servant to this people today, and will serve them and grant them their petition, and speak good words to them, then they will be your servants forever."

Great leaders are great servants – Solomon had lost sight of this in his twilight years. Rehoboam had the opportunity to capture the hearts of the people. This would ensure their allegiance; hence, he would have their support for as long as he was king. Herein was the opportunity to transition to a different style than that of his father and restore hope to the citizens.

Clearly, they needed a change and a migration back to the former years of their youth, before Solomon's ambitious lifestyle.

But, Rehoboam did not listen! He did not understand the difference between privilege and responsibility.

1 Kings 12:8-11 reads:

But he forsook the counsel of the elders which they had given to him, and consulted with the young men who grew up with him and served him.

So he said to them, "What counsel do you give that we may answer this people who have spoken to me, saying "lighten the yoke which your father put on us?"

The young men who grew up with him spoke to him, saying, "Thus you shall say to this people who spoke to you, saying, 'your father made our yoke heavy, now you make it lighter for us!' But you shall speak to them, 'my little finger is thicker than my father's loins! Whereas my father loaded you with a heavy yoke, I will add to your yoke; my father disciplined you with whips, but I will discipline you with scorpions."

Big mistake! Rehoboam's friends had no more wisdom than he did. He assumed that his position of king and ruler would automatically command allegiance and loyalty. He lacked the maturity to understand that every follower is a volunteer. Nobody can be forced to follow. They can be forced to submit, but this does not necessarily make them loyal followers. People don't follow rulers, they follow leaders.

The consequences!

1 Kings 12:16 reads:

When all Israel saw that the king did not listen to them, the people answered the king, saying, "What portion do we have in David? We have no inheritance in the son of Jesse; to your tents, O Israel! Now look after your house, David!" So Israel departed to their tents.

Upon hearing of Rehoboam's leadership strategy, ten of the twelve tribes of Israel decided not to follow. He heeded to advice he wanted to hear, resulting in a revolution. In this eagerness to rule, he lost the opportunity to lead. By posturing himself as a mighty king, he lost his kingdom.[79]

In the book of Ezekiel 34:1-16, God condemned leaders whose interests and focus was more on themselves than the people they were called to serve.

---

[79] Stanley Andy – The Next Generation Leader –Colorado - 2003

Ezekiel 34:8 reads:

"Woe to the shepherds of Israel who only take care of themselves! Should not shepherds take care of the flock? You eat the curds, clothe yourselves with the wool and slaughter the choice animals, but you do not take care of the flock. You have not strengthened the weak or healed the sick or bound up the injured. You have not brought back the strays or searched for the lost. You have ruled them harshly and brutally. So they were scattered because there was no shepherd, and when they were scattered they became food for all the wild animals."

In Zephaniah 3:3, leaders are referred to as evening wolves, which leave nothing for the morning. Meaning that they are devourers until nothing is left.

Zephaniah 3:3 reads:

"Her officials are roaring lions, her rulers are evening wolves, who leave nothing for the morning."

Modern Day Church

The culture of the modern day church has become obsessed with the quest for power. We tend to lean more on appearance than substance. To get ahead we push past anybody and everybody, leaving casualties along the way. It does not matter how we achieve our goals, just as long as we achieve them. The church, in effect, has become a power advocate.

Younger generations – those we refer to as generation Y and millennium generation are leaving institutions that are characterized by a power culture.

These generations, generally, do not have much consideration for allegiance. They have no hesitation in walking away in the event of there being differences or disagreements. However, on the contrary, some will ensure that their point finds its way home. This definitely upsets the status quo.

The previous two generations – we refer to as the baby boomers and silence generation, are familiar with the concept of a slightly older version on leadership principles. A certain element of autocracy was accepted as a norm; hence, the positive ability to adapt is seemingly more evident than generation Y and millennium. Generations Y and millennium will resist power based leadership, purely, because of their culture and environment they are brought up in.

Michael Scott Horton in his book – *The Selling out of the Evangelical Church* states:

Power has become a familiar word in Christian circles. Unlike the small church down the street we used to go to, the new mega-church in the neighboring town has powerful programs, and its buildings often compete with corporate office buildings for the impressive architecture of power.

Or the healing service last week was *powerful,* we all felt the *power.*[80]

Power, authority and control manifest themselves in specific ways within our ministries. Let us examine each of these closely.

Power

The Scribes and Pharisees were deep-set traditionalist. They established systems that had become sacred. Whether it is declaring that bishops are a special class of believers, that the clergy alone has the right to read the Scriptures, or that one's forgiveness comes from a priest and not from God, the pages of history are filled with examples of power abused in the name of Christ.[81]

Abuses of power in our day are often more subtle. Church leadership has become bureaucratic. This tendency will result in the credibility

---

[80] Horton Scott Michael – Selling out of the Evangelical Church – Moody – Chicago - 1992

[81] Rinehart Stacy – Upside down – NavPress – Colorado – 1998

of leaders suffering irreparable damage. People resent being manipulated and managed as mere cogs in an organization.[82]

Howard Snyder in his book *Signs of the Spirit* states that:

Institutions become repositories of vested interests, providing power and security, not easily given up, for those who wield institutional power. Institutions divide people up according to institutional power and status. Generally, institutions make it very clear just where everyone fits – what your place is, and how it compares with those above and below. Institutions define reality in their terms. Right becomes, by definition, what the institutions wants, and evil is to oppose the institution.[83]

This type of inappropriate power exists, very strongly, and must be confronted with the same attitude and vigor with which Jesus confronted the Pharisees. These types of illegitimate controls undermine authentic kingdom leadership principles.

1Timothy 3:1-3 reads:

"Here is a trustworthy saying: If anyone sets his heart on being an overseer, he desires a noble task. Now the overseer must be above reproach, the husband of but one wife, temperate, self-controlled, respectable, hospitable, able to teach, not given to drunkenness, not violent but gentle, not quarrelsome, not a lover of money."

In these passages of scripture, Paul's criteria for ministry are diametrically opposed to any symbol of power. Paul outlines to

---

[82] Means E James – Leadership in Christian Ministry –Grand Rapids -1989
[83] Snyder A Howard – Signs of the Spirit – Grand Rapids – 1989

Timothy specific qualifications for leadership. The crux of every one of these qualification is relationship. Paul told Timothy not to consider anybody for leadership unless he is able to full fill the requirements as above.

Henri Nouwen in his book – *Reflections on Christian Leadership* states:

Much Christian leadership is exercised by people who do not know how to develop healthy, intimate relationships and opted for power and control instead.[84]

The question, in an age so preoccupied by power and image, how much significance do we place on qualities dictated by scripture?

Authority

There is a huge difference between authoritarian and authoritative leadership. Authoritarian leadership types border around a power base structure. Authoritative leadership is an expression of being empowered with knowledge and abilities. This enables a person to speak from a platform of authority void of autocracy.

When Jesus appeared before Pilate - John 19:10-11 states:

"Do you refuse to speak to me?" Pilate said. "Don't you realize I have power either to free you or to crucify you?" Jesus said, "You would have no power over me if it had not given to you from above. Therefore the one who handed me over to you is guilty of a greater sin."

Jesus reinforces the fact that all power comes from God. He has given all authority to Jesus His Son.

Matthew 28: 18 states:

"All authority in heaven and on earth has been given to me."

---

[84] Nouwen Henri – Reflections on Christian Leadership – New York - 1989

Jesus has in turn given this authority to all believers on earth.

Matthew 28:19 reads:

"Therefore, go and make disciples of all nations, baptizing them in the name of the Father, Son and of the Holy Spirit."

Howard Snyder very plainly says that:

The church is a theocracy, not a democracy. It is not a hierarchical theocracy tracing from God down a ladder to a lay peasant. Rather it is a family in which God rules supremely, but kindly and lovingly in a way that builds and affirms each member and makes hierarchy superfluous.

He further states that the church is not a chain of command but a network of love.[85]

Jesus confronted false spiritual authority in his day.

Matthew 23:1 reads:

"The teachers of the law and the Pharisees sit in Moses' seat"

The seat of Moses speaks of a seat of authority. Jesus' confrontation was twofold. First, he pointed out they "seat themselves" in Moses position – a position given only by God. These men had taken authority for themselves; it had not been given to them. Second, the sole basis on which they had grasped this authority was because of their position or rank as Scribes and Pharisees. In other words, their authority was not founded on the fact that they were wise, discerning and true. It was based solely on the fact that they were in charge.[86]

---

[85] Snyder A Howard –Liberating the church – Downers Grove – 1983

[86] Johansen David and Van Vonderen Jeff – The Subtle Power of Spiritual Abuse – Minneapolis – Bethany-1991

Under the New Covenant, the basis for authority is not based on position but the presence of the Holy Spirit in an individual. This is based on humility.

Again we need to look at the example of Paul and Timothy. In the book of 1 Timothy 4:12, Paul did not instruct Timothy to act or perform based on authority. Rather, he told Timothy to be seasoned in speech, conduct, love, faith and purity. He specifically told Timothy to set an example.

In today's world we have power leaders that lead, not through humility, but from a position of authority based on dominant management styles.

Control

Being in control can be both positive and negative. The effects of either one can be easily detected. It boils down to attitudes and motives. It is very comforting to know that a leader that you are serving under has everything under control. While there is absolute need for control, the 'macho' type of a leader can have very negative effects. There may be psychological factors as to why some leaders behave like control freaks. This stems from backgrounds of personal situations and also the lack of leadership knowledge. Insecurity is also another contributor. Leaders feel threatened when people act independently of them. Often times, because of this, the leader has to show them 'who the boss is.'

This is very evident in ministry settings. People are often pressured into conformity. This is a type of illegitimate control. People are manipulated and have to resort to pleasing man because of the fear of being ostracized. Instead of influencing, leaders tend to control through manipulation. Suggestions become insistence. If people do not submit to leadership they are rebellious. Instead of God's vision, the leader's vision now becomes priority.

Controlling others, even those in our spiritual care, is an unattainable goal. People may defer to us for a while. But that will quickly come to an end. To think that we can control people is to believe the lie that got Adam and Eve into so much trouble; they thought they could become like God and be thoroughly independent. Deep down, controllers seem to think just like Adam and Eve, that being in charge will bring them some prize that has thus far eluded them. But control is something we grasp at to keep us from facing our dependency upon God and others.[87]

Author James Mean states:

Often leaders take action that flows not from a serious, spiritual concern for the welfare of the church and a prayerful discernment of God's will, but from their own authoritarian personalities and desire for control. This kind of behavior often provokes a spirit of rebellion or hostility in the congregation, and it becomes impossible to maintain proper respect and deference.[88]

Leaders ordained, mandated and sanctioned by God should not be power seekers. They have absolutely no need for creating an impression. The twelve disciples knew that they were not to behave in a manner like the Gentiles did.

Sometimes "vision" is confused with "personal ambition." Such a vision relies on worldly means. A vision that depends upon the continued presence and positional power is not authored by God.[89]

Visionaries operating in the flesh promote messages like this:

- "If you are not getting my vision, you are not listening to God, or you are spiritually immature and inferior."

- "This is the only true spiritual vision around here. If you have another vision, we will be unequally yoked."

---

[87] Rinehart Stacy – Upside down – NavPress – Colorado – 1998

[88] Means E James – Leadership in Christian Ministry –Grand Rapids -1989 Means E James -

[89] Rinehart Stacy – Upside down – NavPress – Colorado – 1998

- "You must remember that you are extensions of the senior pastor and are therefore responsible for achieving his vision."
- "You must follow my vision and strategy – it's been proven to work."[90]

Leaders and their followers must constantly discern if the power, authority, and control is coming from a position or the Holy Spirit working through a humble servant. Is the focus always upon the leader and his vision? Or are people consistently directed to Christ? Paul offers a litmus test: "For we do not preach ourselves but Christ Jesus as Lord, and ourselves as your bond-servants for Jesus' sake" (2 Corinthians 4:5). Any other approach to leadership can lead to serious forms of authoritarian abuse. [91]

Structure of Power

Structures can either foster or hinder a ministry. Alternately, it can be a curse or a blessing. A structure has no life of its own. In a power based structure, the voice of authority comes from a leader or combination of leaders and the ministry structures they represent. The primary focus for leaders is responsibility with hearing from God and deciding the direction of the ministry. These leaders filter God's voice and then make demands on people to full fill their vision. People end up serving the leadership and the structure. Questioning leadership is seemed as though God is questioned.[92]

According to Stacy Rinehart – in his book – *Upside Down* - Power base structures usually emphasize two things:[93]

- Roles and Position – In power based ministries structures; you know where you stand in the order of things. The organizational chart may not be visibly printed, but little

---

[90] Rinehart Stacy – Upside down – NavPress – Colorado – 1998
[91] Ibid
[92] Rinehart Stacy – Upside down – NavPress – Colorado – 1998
[93] Ibid

happens unless sufficient position or power makes it happen. The leader's vision is carried out by everyone "below" him. Decisions, new initiatives, and long range direction flow down from a select few, with little input from others. An emphasis on role and position, in effect, resorts to ministry by the priesthood of the elite, not by all believers. How different is the New Testament model! There, men and women emerged from Judaism, having lived amidst the Roman military system, with its emphasis on rank and position. Yet, those early believers operated as members of the body, in mutual submission to one another and Christ without adapting to their surrounding structures.

- Control and boundaries – If leaders subtly present themselves as "the anointed" or as somehow superior in their understanding of God and His Word, and they use that image to demand loyalty, they create an unholy structure for control.

A leader's estimate of humanity is revealed by the way he leads and structures his ministry. If he has a low estimate of humanity, he leads with an iron fist and structures the ministry for tight control. If he views peoples as sheep, he structures the ministry to gain control of the flock. If the church members are merely lay people, he structures for the clerics to be in charge. If he sees men and women as tools to be used in accomplishing a task or vision, he structures them as employees and puts them to work on the assembly line of ministry production.[94]

The challenge facing leadership is to create an environment, where people are encouraged to live out God's purpose in their lives. Ministry structures must not be allowed to degenerate into forms devoid of original functions.

---

[94] Ibid

Power structures create or perpetuate the subtle artificial ways of using or abusing people, rather than serving them.[95]

Jesus never said or did anything to indicate that structure and organization could serve to protect God's people. Shepherds and servants, yes, they would be needed, but He never talked about structure. It is necessary… but for protecting His people He had something far more trustworthy – the Holy Spirit.[96]

Whose Kingdom Are We Building

The unanimous response here would be God's Kingdom. This is, or should be, any leader's response. Our primary responsibility is to build God's Kingdom. While this may be our priority, subconsciously, we, to an extent build our own empires. This is largely due to having a sense of security as most leaders are dependent on their organization for an income. There is a shift in reasoning here. Leaders who are called by God should be dependent on Him to sustain them. Unless we cling to the kingdom of God and its values, we'll quickly fall into the trap of trying to build our own kingdom while calling it God's.[97]

The kingdom has been misunderstood throughout the ages, despite being one of the focal points of Jesus. The Kingdom is God's sovereign rule for all eternity over creation. Unless we come to the point of this realization, we will continue to divert from the core responsibility of building God's Kingdom.

Jesus told His disciples that they needed to do His work so that the kingdom may grow.

The Book of Mark 16:15-18 reads:

---

[95] Rinehart Stacy – Upside down – NavPress – Colorado – 1998
[96] Peterson Jim – Church Without Walls – NavPress – Colorado - 1992
[97] Rinehart Stacy – Upside down – NavPress – Colorado – 1998

He said to them, "Go into all the world and preach the good news to all creation.

Whoever believes and is baptized will be saved, but whoever does not believe will be condemned. And these signs will accompany those who believe: In my Name they will drive out demons; they will pick up snakes with their hands; and will not hurt them at all; they will place their hands on sick people and they will get well."

The building of the Kingdom of God became an integral part of the disciples' mission. They began preaching the gospel and starting ministries.

The book of Acts 28:31 reads:

"Boldly and without hindrance he preached the kingdom of God and taught about the Lord Jesus Christ."

This message began to filter down to the Apostles. Paul declared that all of history will culminate with one act-when Christ "delivers up the kingdom to God the Father, when He has abolished all rule and all authority and power" (1Corinthians 15:24).[98]

These are simple, fundamental truths that we can easily overlook. When our focus shifts away from these truths, we begin to build our kingdom rather that God's kingdom.

Recognizing Limitations

Some of this was covered in chapter four - Know Thyself.

In the early stages of ministry, I had to be multi-skilled. I had to teach Sunday School, not just teach but gather the children from their homes, teach and return them to their homes. I convened the morning service and sometimes preached. Later in the afternoon, I took charge of the youth meetings. On some days, apart from doing all of these,

---

[98] Ibid

I also drove the church bus. This led me to think that I was a Jack of all trades. This was necessary at the time, as there was a lack of resources and manpower.

Presently, for someone to do this is unthinkable. Times have changed and we are now dealing with a different generation of people. Therefore, it is necessary for people like me to realize my limitations. At one stage I used to be able to do a lot, now, the work has to be shared. If I attempted to do what I used to, I would not be able to accomplish much. Other ministers of the old school need to also realize this. Here again, the advice that Moses received from Jethro –Exodus chapter 18 - plays an important part. We simply cannot do everything. We will stress and result in a burn out. Much of this has already been discussed under stress management.

The greatest set-back suffered by most ministers is the ability to let go. For some reason, if they let go, it would seem as though everything will fall to pieces. There is also a fear of allowing the infiltration of new blood that may outshine the old type ministry style. Off course, no one will admit this. This is the exact reason why so many ministries are stifled. No real or significant numerical growth. No change in spiritual growth and maturity. The same re-cycled sermons are preached time and time again. No noted maturity in their leadership. Invariably, you will see that the leadership has somewhat molded themselves after their leader. They tend to preach the same, speak the same and behave like their leader. Pleasing their leader is of utmost importance.

This gives birth to religion. The activities of the church become more important than family life, sometimes, more important than God. The life of the entire leadership is surrounded by the leader and church activities. Absolutely no attention is paid to children, husbands and wives. Family values are diminished. This then gives birth to rebellion. Young people turn against their elders. Teenage pregnancy is the order of the day. Many of the weddings performed are due to premarital sex resulting in pregnancy. As a result of young marriages, problems develop between couples resulting in other sinful influences creeping in. Is there a problem? Yes!!! Try to get the leader to understand this.

Some leaders feel that they know it all. Instead of offering proper counseling, they make matters worse. Some cases need specialized counseling. This requires certain expertise. Unfortunately, even senior leaders sometimes lack this expertise. To request anybody other than the senior leader is an indictment or underestimation of his abilities. This has far reaching implications. If you follow this route, prepare to be ostracized.

This gives birth to negative influences. Some people get programmed by these negative experiences. This leads them to perform negatively and negative self-concepts show up through the feeling of inadequacy, a stifling of ability resulting in diminished values and achievements. To fix this will require the power to re-construct self-image through a process of reverse learning. Meaning, there has to be a de-construction and re-construction of mind-sets, and re-establishment of value systems of self-worth.

Limitations are when you are able to recognize them. Every person is gifted, some are multi-gifted. Every gift has limitations. Teachers must teach, Prophets must prophecy, Evangelists must preach etc. There will be some cross-over, but, rarely, does one person have the ability to practice all of the gifts

The book of Corinthians 12:4-11 reads:

> **"There are different types of gifts, but the same spirit. There are different kinds of service, but the same Lord. There are different kinds of working, but the same God works all of them in all men. Now to each one the manifestation of the spirit is given for the common good. To one there is given through the Spirit the message of wisdom, to another the message of knowledge, by means of the same Spirit, to another miraculous powers, to another prophecy, to another, distinguishing between spirits, to another speaking in different kinds of tongues,**

and to still another, the interpretation of tongues. All these are the work of one and the same Spirit, and he gives them to each one, just as He determines."

One's gifting is internal. The expression of that gifting has external influences. Therefore, there is a need to operate, primarily, within the confines of that gifting. What is the result when we do not acknowledge our limitations?

Stacy Rhinehart gives us some interesting conclusions.[99]

First, this will have a definite effect on the body of Christ. Failure to operate within our limits will take a physical, mental, emotional and spiritual toll. (refer to my early ministry days as discussed).

Second, omni-competence prevents the proper functioning of other members. Living within the range of one's gifts fosters deference to other members of the body. This provides others opportunity to lead and develop.

While operating within our God-given boundaries, it makes room for interdependence among other believers. It is the same principle of living in obedience. Gifting is sovereign, designed to glorify God, through maximizing our contributions. There are two primary reasons to be careful of, pride and the quest for prominence and control.

The more we live within our gifts and our spheres of ministry, the more we will see Christ manifested through the work of the Holy Spirit. In this way the grace of God spreads through us.

Philip Greenslade comments:

Paul wanted to reassure the Corinthians about himself and his team. "That we will not boast beyond our measure, but within the measure of the sphere which God has apportioned us." …. In fact, our authority has greater weight, Paul says, because we are not

---

[99] Rinehart Stacy – Upside down – NavPress – Colorado – 1998

overextending ourselves. Pressed to undertake commitments on every side, today's leaders would do well to take this to heart. Knowing our limitations is a saving grace.[100]

If we live according to our limits, we will not overestimate our importance or strive to be indispensable. True humility forces us to recognize our limitations.

If we are faithful stewards of our own gifts, we will be most comfortable serving God in a team context. Tasks and responsibilities are spread around, with each person being recognized for their unique contribution.

The old system typified by dominance, rank and positional authority are ineffective in the long term. Leading as the world leads, through manipulation, personal charisma or subtle intimidation must die hard in every one of us.

Christ and the early church members modeled such risky servant leadership – risking and giving something greater than themselves. Serving others was of paramount importance. They did not depend on numbers or convenience. Today this is dependent on a commitment to full fill a calling as a leader whose prime interest should be – interest in people. Timothy was known for a genuine interest in people.

Philippians 2: 19-21 reads:

> **"I hope in the Lord Jesus to send Timothy to you soon, so that I also may be cheered when I receive news about you. I have no one else like him, who takes a genuine interest in your welfare. For everyone looks out for his own interests, not those of Jesus Christ."**

Power leadership can also be termed as a type of "corrupt" leadership. This is not corrupt as we know it to be, but in a form of self-

---

[100] Greenslade Philip – Leadership, Greatness and Servanthood – Minneapolis - 1984

engagement with one's own self. When this is the case, its influence will destroy the moral fiber of the people. We have preachers using pulpits as a platform to vent their frustration. They have anger attacking personalities. This is a vile action, as this is one way communication. Hence, people cannot respond to threats and allegations or engage in discussion. The unfortunate aspect of all of this is that, even though we should be careful not to be defensive, whatever is said, unless challenged, becomes the message to the listeners. These leaders are no longer capable of expounding the Word with power and insight.

Chapter 11

Technology of a Leader

The Bible consists of many examples of leaders, both good and bad. This is also very evident in the world today. History also records many leaders. Not all of them are role models or examples to be followed. Hence, by virtue of having the title, or being called a leader does not necessarily mean that positive attributes emanates from this person. Through custom and practice, we often expect any association with a leader to be more positive than negative.

In order to facilitate a process of thinking positively of leaders, I have chosen a few influential biblical characters, analyzed their style and have highlighted some of their character traits that could be beneficial. The ultimate choice of all examples, the best example that epitomized the optimum traits of leadership is the example of Jesus. This example is also included in this chapter. Most of these leadership styles constitute a study on their own. However, these basic outlines will help us to understand leadership technologies better. Technology, meaning, a type and style that is unique and is exhibited by these biblical characters, which produced great exploits for God.

There is a synergy in all of these examples that will ultimately bring further definition to the title leadership.

For better understanding of all these examples, biblical reference is absolutely necessary.

Nehemiah's Technology

His Character

Nehemiah was an inspiring leader who God used in a short space of time to accomplish amazing results. God was able to bring out true leadership values in Nehemiah, largely due to the quality of Nehemiah's character.

Nehemiah's strength was derived from his prayer life. He sought God and the will of God in his life because of his ability to live a life of prayer. Prayer was a lifestyle he adopted. Therefore, when he heard the plight of the emigrants in Jerusalem, the first thing he did was to approach the Throne of Grace to which he was no stranger.

Nehemiah 1:4 reads:

"When I heard these things, I sat down and wept. For some days I mourned and fasted and prayed before God in heaven."

As a result of his ardent prayer life, he always displayed courage in the face of danger.

The glaring evidences in this verse are:

- He has the capacity to listen
- His ability to be empathetic
- His acceptance of responsibility to get involved

Nehemiah 6:11 reads:

But I said, "Should a man like me run away? Or should one like me go into the temple to save his life? I will not go."

His genuine concern for the welfare of others was recognized by his enemies.

Nehemiah 2:10 reads:

"When Sanballat the Horonite and Tobiah the Ammonite official heard about this, they were very much disturbed that someone had come to promote the welfare of the Israelites."

Nehemiah identified with his people – a real quality of a leader. He was also a man of foresight. He knew that opposition was arising against him. He secured letters from the king for a safe passage in order to accomplish his task. – Nehemiah 2:10.

He was also able to make clear decisions. He did not avoid confrontation or put off a tough call. He made impartial decisions; he did not show favoritism.[101]

He listened to grievances and took the necessary action. He was empathetic – he let people "weep on his shoulder." He sympathized with others.

He was also a realist. He understood the workings of the real world. Therefore in Chapter 4 –verse 9 - "We prayed to our God and posted a guard day and night"

He accepted responsibility and followed through all assignments – until the job was done. He was a vigorous administrator, a calm crisis manager, a fearless initiator, a courageous decision maker, and a persevering leader. He was resolute in the face of threats and vigilant against treachery – a leader who won and held the full confidence of his followers.[102]

His Methods

Nehemiah was a morale builder and a motivational leader. He redirected the thought process of his team by focusing on the greatness of God.

Nehemiah 2:20 reads:

I answered them by saying, "The God of heaven will give us success. We his servants will start re-building, but as for you, you have no share in Jerusalem or any claim or historic right to it."

Nehemiah 8:10 reads:

---

[101] Sanders J Oswald – Spiritual Leadership – Moody Press – Chicago - 1999

[102] Sanders J Oswald – Spiritual Leadership – Moody Press – Chicago - 1999

"Nehemiah said, "Go and enjoy choice food and sweet drinks, and send some to those who have nothing prepared. This day is sacred to our Lord. Do not grieve, for the joy of the Lord is your strength."

Nehemiah discovered that one of the best ways to keep people confidant in the face of opposition was to build faith. This brought about a great sense of joy. Prior to this the people were discouraged and demoralized. He restored hope by building faith and directing them to the providence of God.

Nehemiah 2:18 reads:

"I also told them about the gracious hand of God upon me and what the king had said to me. They replied, "let us start building. So they began this good work."

The result of Nehemiah's ability to establish confidence caused him to stamp authority.

Like everything in life, Nehemiah also was aware of their weakness.

In one instance the people were tired and discouraged. Opponents were making life miserable (4:10-18). Garbage was piling up and hampering progress. Nehemiah first directed their vision to God, then put them under arms and deployed them at strategic points. He harnessed the strength of the family unit, ordering half a family to work while the other half stood guard and rested. The people recovered their courage as Nehemiah solved real problems through decisive action.[103]

In another instance, the people were disillusioned by the greed of their own rich brothers (5:1-15). Most people lived on mortgaged lands; some had sold children as slaves to meet expenses. "Neither is it in

---

[103] Sanders J Oswald – Spiritual Leadership – Moody Press – Chicago - 1999

our power to redeem them; for other men have our lands and vineyards" (v. 5)[104]

Nehemiah listened to the problems of the people and sympathized with their suffering. He rebuked the nobles (5:7) and appealed for immediate relief. (5: 11). So effective was negotiations that the reply of the nobles was simply, "We will do as you say" (v 12)[105]

Nehemiah recovered the authority of the Word of God in the lives of the people (8:1-8).

This made his reforms possible. He restored the Feast of Tabernacles, which had not been observed since the time of Joshua. He led the people to repentance through the reading of the law (9:3-5). He purified the temple of pagan influence (13:4-9). He encouraged tithing, established Sabbath rest, forbade intermarriage with pagan foreigners, and so recovered the special identity of Israel as God's chosen people.[106]

Nehemiah also had the ability to organize projects and people. He always surveyed a situation (2:11-16). He established the key objectives and assigned responsibilities to leaders (7:1-3). He gave recognition to subordinates (3:1-32). He practiced a wise delegation of authority.

Nehemiah 7:2 reads:

"I put in charge of Jerusalem my brother Hananai, along with Hananaiah the commander of the citadel"

He had a high standard for the people he chose to be key players. He chose Hananaiah "because he was a man of integrity and feared God

---

[104] Sanders J Oswald – Spiritual Leadership – Moody Press – Chicago - 1999
[105] Ibid
[106] Ibid

more than most men do." All of this opened the leadership potential of others.[107]

Nehemiah faced up to opposition without forcing a violent confrontation. He took insults, innuendo, intimidation, and treachery. He walked through it with his head high and his eyes wide open, with much prayer (4:9). He sometimes ignored adversary. He always took precautions (v 16). He never allowed opposition to deflect his energy from the central task. He always kept faith in God (v 20).[108]

The true test of spiritual leadership is the achievement of its objective. In the case of Nehemiah the record is clear:

"So the wall was completed" (6:15)

An analysis of all of the leadership techniques and styles expressed by Nehemiah, three principles stand out:

- Co-Ordination – his strategic planning, delegation of duties and team effort.

- Co-Operation – a gathering together of men from different works of life and places. This includes Priests, Levites, Rulers, Gatekeepers, common people etc. He explored synergies, created a common platform that gave true meaning to teamwork.

- Commendation – This is a key principle of motivation. He acknowledged their zeal and enthusiasm. He stood by them through rough times and good times. In spite of all the opposition and valley experiences he acknowledged an effort, whether great or small.

---

[107] Ibid
[108] Ibid

David's Technology

David was the youngest of the Old Testament characters that brought worth and definition to a new type leader. Even though he was a shepherd boy, he was a leader in waiting. He had inherent skills born within him to eventually lead an entire nation. Not only to be a leader, but a King. As was customary, the King's son, Jonathan would be the natural heir to replace the King. David's ascension to the throne was somewhat beyond anyone's comprehension. It was God ordained. In spite of being God ordained, David had to express qualities based on his own intellect, to prove that he was destined for greatness. The single most evident factor of his leadership ability was not his talents or even the fact he was called by God. This evidence was seen in his courage. One display of his courage, be it out of innocence or ignorance, brought him national fame. This ultimately led to a historical and national significance for the nation of Israel.

He fought for what he believed in. He fought with vigor to guard that which was entrusted to him. This was evidenced by his ability to stand against lions and wolves, to protect his sheep. He placed value on his responsibilities, even if it was just shepherding. He was not highly esteemed by his father Jesse or his brothers, especially, in adding value to the family "business". He was given the most menial of tasks. Yet he was a King in the making.

The event that brought definition to David was the stalemate between of the armies of Israel and the Philistines - **1 Samuel – 17: 38-52**. He had the ability to overcome with great ease, what the army of Israel thought was a death wish. The army of Saul was terrified with the might and strength of Goliath. David was overcome with the supremacy of the Eternal God. Saul's army thought Goliath too big to hit. David thought Goliath too big to miss! The irony is that Goliath was dressed for battle in the physical. David was dressed for battle in the spiritual.

This legendry display of courage and determination catapulted David from mediocre to fame. He certainly got Saul's attention. He later went on to be Saul's military strategist. He also played the harp that soothed Saul's restlessness (1 Samuel 18:10). His military precision won many victories. The relationship between Saul and David became estranged when David was perceived as a threat to Saul. Saul was paranoid in his quest to kill David. During these turbulent times, Jonathan, Saul's son became a covenant friend with David. Jonathan warned David of Saul's intentions. In all of this turmoil, David esteemed Saul as king. He had numerous opportunities to kill Saul, but did not. (1 Samuel 24)

Of course, we cannot ignore the divine destiny factor that was preordained. He was in line to be King, even though he was not the son of Saul.

David was not only courageous and generous, but a force to be reckoned with. As always, the bible does not idealize its hero's. The faults and failings of leaders are recorded alongside their amazing exploits and demonstration of humble service.[109] David was no exception.

In the book of 2 Samuel 11:1 to 12:10 – we read the most disparaging chapter of David's life. This time period was characterized by sexual lust, adultery and finally, in the vain attempt to hide his sin, complicity to murder. Indeed, a terrible episode, but in light of David's confession and repentance, God forgave him. Failure is not final. David's story in particular demonstrates why any analysis of leadership cannot ignore or deny the human factor, and it also shows humility is a necessary prerequisite for any leader.[110]

In spite of his shortfalls, David was a strategist. He was able to surround himself with mighty men of valor – (2 Samuel 23 /1 Chronicles 12). These men, led by David brought victory that previously was never witnessed in history.

---

[109] Gibbs Eddie – Leadership Next – Intervarsity Press – UK - 2005
[110] Ibid

Paul's Technology

The Apostle Paul was one of the greatest leaders that ever lived. He had the ability and the knowledge to address people from every facet of life. He was able to capture the attention of any group, be it kings or ordinary people. He studied under one of the most influential leaders of his time named, Gamaliel. He was able to overcome both cultural and racial barriers. A person's wealth or poverty, social status or intellect had no bearing on Paul's concern. All people were his concern. In addition to his academic intellect, he enjoyed the illumination and inspiration of the Holy Spirit.

Paul was Timothy's mentor. He equipped Timothy as they travelled together (Acts 16:1-5). When Paul found that Timothy was qualified to do ministry, he left him to lead the church of Ephesus (1Timothy 1:3). Paul wrote a letter to Timothy and told him to entrust what he had learned from Paul to faithful men who would also "be qualified to teach others" (2 Timothy 2:2). Paul told Timothy to find reliable men to train others.[111]

Paul, especially in his writings to Timothy, clearly spells out the requirements for leadership. He not only spells it out, but also set the standards.

The book of 1 Timothy 3:2-7 reads:

"Now the overseer must be above reproach, the husband of but one wife, temperate, self-controlled, respectable, hospitable, able to teach, not given to drunkenness, not violent but gentle, not quarrelsome, not a lover of money. He must manage his own family well and see that his children obey him with proper respect. (If anyone does not know how to manage his own family, how can he take care of God's church?) He must not be a recent convert, or he may become conceited and fall under the same judgment as the devil. He must also have a good reputation with

---

[111] Wilkers C. Gene-Jesus Leadership-Lifeway Press-Illinois-1996

outsiders, so that he will not fall into disgrace and into the devil's trap."

These verses of scripture spell out the qualifications for spiritual leadership. J. Oswald Sanders in his book Spiritual Leadership best describes this under the following

Social Qualifications

With respect to relationships within the church, the leader is to be above reproach. His life is an open book and therefore offers no grounds for reproach or indictment of wrong doing. His adversaries can find no opening for smear campaigns, rumour mongering or gossiping.

With respect to relationships outside the church, he has to enjoy a good reputation. This has been discussed in Chapter four. There must be no gap or difference in the public and private life of a leader. In spite of any criticism, and there will be, all will respect the high ideals of his Christian character. Because of this he will become a role model for those who are aspiring to be leaders in the future. The character of the leader should command the respect of the unbeliever, inspire his confidence, and arouse his aspiration. His living example is much more potent.[112]

Moral Qualifications

Moral principles common to the Christian life are under constant attack. Once again, the Christian leader must be blameless and above reproach. Faithfulness to one marriage partner is absolute. His morality and integrity must be unquestionable. He must be a temperate person, not addicted to alcohol. There must be no secret indulgence.[113]

---

[112] Sanders J Oswald – Spiritual Leadership – Moody Press – Chicago - 1999
[113] Ibid

Mental Qualifications

A leader must be prudent, a person with sound judgment. This principle describes "the well-balanced state of mind resulting from habitual self-restraint" – the inner character that comes from daily self – discipline. This quality is called "reason's girdle and passion's bridle."[114] A Christian leader who possesses a sound mind has control of every part of his personality, habits, and passions.

He must be respectable. An orderly life is as a result of an orderly mind. Therefore, the life of the leader should reflect the beauty and orderliness of God. The leader must be able to teach. This creates opportunities to help and develop others. This responsibility must be reflected through a blameless life.

Personality Qualifications

A leader must be kind and gentle by nature, not a person who thrives on controversy. He must have the ability to correct and redress situations. He must also be actively considerate, not passive, always seeking a peaceful solution. He must be able to diffuse volatile situations.

He must be able to show hospitality. The ministry should never be seen as a burden but a privilege of service. When Paul wrote the book of Timothy, inns were dirty and had an immoral atmosphere. Visiting Christians depended on open doors of hospitality with their Christian brothers and sisters.

The love of money disqualifies a person from leadership. Financial reward cannot enter a leader's mind in the exercise of ministry. Appointments should not be accepted on remuneration, rather with the prime focus of service.

Here is a great example:

---

[114] Barclay Williams – Letters to Timothy and Titus –Edinburgh - 1960

Before going to Madely, John Fletcher was told by his benefactor, Mr. Hill, that he could have a position in Dunham in Cheshire, where "the parish is small, the duty light, and the income good," Moreover, it was "in fine sporting country."

"Alas, sir," replied Fletcher, "Dunham will not suit me. There is too much money and too little labor."

"It's a pity to decline such a living," said Hill. "Would you like Madeley?"

"That, sir, would be the very place for me."

And in that church the man who cared nothing for money had a remarkable ministry, still being felt in this generation.[115]

Domestic Qualifications

A Christian leader who is married must demonstrate the ability to "manage his own family well and see that his children obey him with proper respect" (1Timothy 3:4).

Paul urges a well ordered home where there is mutual respect and harmony. Failure to keep homes in order will prevent a leader from giving off their full potential.

The spouse must be equally involved in the ministry by sharing the leader's aspirations and make the necessary sacrifices. Many gifted leaders have lost spiritual effectiveness because of uncooperative spouses. How can a leader be able to manage a ministry if he cannot maintain the required order at home? Can hospitality be offered if children carry on without restraint? Can a ministry to other families be effective if one's own family is in disarray?[116]

---

[115] Fletcher John William-was the vicar of Madeley in Shopshire- joined the Methodist movement within the Church of England – worked among the coal miners.

[116] Sanders J Oswald – Spiritual Leadership – Moody Press – Chicago - 1999

While a leader is caring for ministry, his family must not be neglected. They are his primary and personal responsibility. The discharge of one duty in God's kingdom does not excuse us from another. There is time for every legitimate duty. Paul implies that a person's ability to lead at home is a strong indicator of his readiness to lead in ministry.[117]

Maturity

Maturity is an absolute essential in good leadership. Paul makes it very clear that a novice or a new convert must not be pushed into leadership. Like a growing plant that needs to develop its root, the process must not be hurried.

In 1Timothy 3:10, Paul urges that they must be tested – referring to the qualifications for deacons. The church in Ephesus was a decade old when Timothy became its pastor. There were many men of experience in it, hence, Paul's insistence that the new minister must be mature.

Paul warns that a person who is not ready for leadership, "may become conceited and fall under the same judgment as the devil" (1 Timothy 3:6). A new convert does not possess the stability to lead people wisely. It is unwise to give key positions too early even to those who manifest promising talent. A novice suddenly placed in authority over others, faces the danger of an inflated ego.[118]

Paul did not appoint elders in every place on his first missionary journey. He sometimes waited till later when he questions spiritual development (Acts 14:23). Timothy was converted during Paul's first journey, but not ordained until the second journey.[119]

---

[117] Sanders J Oswald – Spiritual Leadership – Moody Press – Chicago - 1999

[118] Ibid

[119] Hendrikson William-1 and 2 Timothy and Titus – London - 1959

Paul also gave Titus the exact same instruction as Timothy. Remember, as discussed in Leadership Traits, Titus had the responsibility to appoint leaders in Crete.

Maturity is shown in spirit and vision. Paul is an excellent example of this.

The importance of these requirements for leadership is recognized in the secular world.

The Greek Philosopher, Onosander, who wrote on the duties of a general, described the ideal field commander: "He must be prudently self-controlled, sober, frugal, enduring in toil, intelligent, without love of money, neither young or old, if possible the father of a family, able to speak competently, and of good reputation."[120]

If the world demands such qualities, how much more value should we place on appointment of leaders.

Peter's Technology

1 Peter 5:1-7 reads

"To the elders among you, I appeal as a fellow elder, a witness of Christ's sufferings and one who will also share in the glory to he revealed: Be shepherds of God's flock that is under your care, serving as overseers-not because you must, but because you are willing, as God wants you to be; not greedy for money, but eager to serve; not lording it over those entrusted to you, but being examples to the flock. And when the Chief Shepherd appears, you will receive the crown of glory that will never fade away.

Young men, in the same way be submissive to those who are older. All of you, clothe yourselves with humility toward one another, because, "God opposes the proud, but gives grace to the humble."

---

[120] Barclay Williams – Letters to Timothy and Titus –Edinburgh - 1960

Humble yourselves, therefore, under God's mighty hand, that He may lift you up in due time. Cast all your anxiety on Him because he cares for you."

Peter was a natural leader of the apostolic band. He had great influence as a leader because others seemed to do what he did and go where he went. In the first century, leaders had no models or tradition from which to draw regarding church growth. They followed the trial and error pattern and thus progressed as they went along. The primary leadership responsibilities fell on a handful of men of which Peter was a part. As far as leadership principles were concerned, the only model, left as an example was Jesus. Acts 6:1-7 reflects how structure was built giving church growth a true definition.

In 1 Peter 5:2 – See that your flock is properly fed and cared for – he urges that this is the prime responsibility of a Christian leader. Peter writes from a position of a fellow elder, not from a position of high authority. He also writes as a witness. Therefore, he is able to identify with those that he writes to. He also writes as a witness to the sufferings of Christ. He looks across to others not down at them.

He deals with the leader's motivation. The spiritual leader is to approach the ministry willingly, not by coercion. Leaders in Peter's day faced many challenges, no different from today. He urged the leaders to face these challenges and serve not from a sense of duty but from love.

William Barclay, in his book – *The Letters of Peter and Jude* captures best this idea.

Peter says to the leaders, "Shepherd your people like God." Just as Israel is God's special allotment, the people we have to serve in the church or anywhere else are our special allotment; and our whole attitude to them must be the attitude of God; we must shepherd them like God. What visions opens out! What an idea! And what a condemnation! It is our task to show people the forbearance of God, the forgiveness of God, the seeking love of God, the limitless service of God.[121]

Peter also addresses the issue of money. The leader has to understand that service, not money is the priority. Peter warns in 1 Peter 5:2 – do not work as one "greedy for money." He perhaps had Judas in mind whose passion for money led to his fall. Leaders will be called to formulate policy, to set budgets and decide priorities, and to deal with property. None of this will be handled well if personal motives bloom in the background.[122]

Paul Rees in his book – *Triumphant in Trouble* – suggests that the greed Peter warns against extends beyond money to fame and prestige, which are sometimes a more insidious temptation. Whether for fame or fortune, avarice cannot coexist with leadership in the church.[123]

J.H. Jowett, in his book – *The Epistles of Peter* adds the following:

"I am not sure which of the two occupies the lower sphere, he who hungers for money or he who thirsts for applause."

"A preacher may dress and smooth his message to court the public sheers, and labours in other spheres may bid for prominence, for imposing print, for grateful recognition. All this unfits us for our task. It destroys perception of the needs and perils of the sheep."[124]

A leader must not be dictatorial. 1 Peter 5:3 states "Not lording it over those entrusted to you." A domineering manner, and unbridled ambition, an offensive strut, a tyrant's talk - no attitude could be less fit for one who claims to be a servant of the Son of God.[125]

---

[121] Barclay William – The Letters of Peter and Jude- Edinburgh – 1958
[122] Sanders J Oswald – Spiritual Leadership – Moody Press – Chicago - 1999
[123] Rees S. Paul- Triumphant in Trouble – Marshall, Morgan and Scott- London
[124] Jowett J.H. – The Epistles of Peter – Hodder & Stoughton -London
[125] Sanders J Oswald – Spiritual Leadership – Moody Press – Chicago - 1999

A leader must be worthy example for the people. "Being examples to the flock" (1 Peter 5:3).

In the previous chapter, this was the similar advice Paul gave Timothy – "But set an example for the believers in speech, in life, in love, in faith and in purity" (1 Timothy 4:12).

Peter teaches that need for a shepherd's heart. They should always remember that they are overseers of God's flock. Jesus is the Chief Shepherd. We are merely assistants working under His delegated authority.

The leader must be clothed "with humility" (1 Peter 5:5). In verse 5 Peter urges leaders to act humble in relating to others. In verse 6, he challenges leaders to react humbly to the discipline of God. "Therefore humbly submit to God's strong hand".

Peter concludes with the mention of heavenly reward: "When the Chief Shepherd appears, you will receive the crown of glory that will never fade away" (1 Peter 5:4)

We are not alone. Peter encourages us to "Cast all your anxiety on him because he cares for you" (1 Peter 5:7). While caring for the flock can sometimes prove to be heavy burden, we have a shoulder to lean on.

Jesus' Technology

As earlier indicated, leaders of the first century had no model or traditions from which to follow or draw from. Consequently, they had no choice but to develop a structure as they went along. Hence, the primary leadership responsibilities fell on a handful of men whose role model was Jesus.

How it was possible that the early church developed and deployed so many leaders within such a short space of time is mind boggling.

As earlier stated, the example of Jesus was not only spoken of, but exhibited in both His teachings and lifestyle. He negated status as a symbol of prominence and superiority. He represented a life style characterized by humility and simplicity. He never advocated a hierarchical dynasty, but always practiced a relational type model.

Centuries later, in spite of globalization of the information age, His influences still somewhat, seem to be absolutely pertinent to our current day and age.

Jesus' technology of leadership development is summarized in Mark 3.

Mark 3:14-15 reads

"He appointed twelve – designating them apostles – that they might be with him and that He might send them out to preach and to have authority to drive our demons."

After the appointing of leaders, there are two areas of importance:

- The first being "that they might be with him" – signifying a transformational training program within a context of a spiritual environment involving a relation with God through Himself. Also, a relational context, involving relationship with Himself, a mature leader type and others, which involves the other disciples or learners.
- The second being within an experimental context, involving challenging assignments and diverse learning opportunities.

In summary, the five dynamics used are relations, both experimental and instructional.

- Spiritual life is nurtured
- Relational capacities are strengthened
- Character is developed
- Calling is clarified

- Leadership capacities are built

Apart from the twelve disciples He appointed, He also appointed another seventy.

Luke 10:1 reads

"After these things the Lord appointed seventy others also, and sent them two by two before His face into every city and place where He Himself was about to go."

Jesus' leadership strategy encompasses holistic principles pertaining to transformational dynamics. All of these involved constant coaching, monitoring and constructive engagement

Based on the premise that leaders build leaders, Jesus built a few main leaders and through these leaders the world would be affected through the birth of the church. Paul and other leaders in the New Testament pursued this model of leadership development.

2 Timothy 2:2 reads:

"the things you have heard me say in the presence of many witnesses entrust to reliable men who will also be qualified to teach others"

This formula ensures continuity and multiplication of leadership development.

Servanthood the Measure of Greatness

History records great men and women whose influences still live on today. Some have achieved greatness with strength and valor whilst others, through pain, suffering and personal sacrifice. Of all the leaders that existed and exist never has there been a record of any person who has closely resembled our Lord Jesus Christ. His example has left a legacy that has lived and will live for centuries to come, even until the end of age. His display of lifestyle and behavior encompasses every facet of life. There are no questions or debate that will argue otherwise. He was a perfect example that continues to be relevant in our day and age.

Jesus was driven by a sense of destiny. He came to earth in obedience and under took a ministry of both, salvation and identification. He came to seek and save those that were lost (John 14:34). He came not only, to announce God's reign, but to inaugurate it. John the Baptist propagated God's Kingdom.[126]

Servant Leadership was modeled by Jesus in the upper room, when he washed the feet of the disciples (John 13:1-17). This is an example Jesus intended for his disciples to emulate.

John 13: 14-15 reads:

"Now that I your Lord and Teacher, have washed your feet, you should wash one another's feet. I have set you an example that you should do as I have done unto you."

This event caused great embarrassment among the disciples. In the Jewish household, foot washing was regarding as the most menial of all tasks.

His display epitomizes life in its reality. Again I must emphasize, even at the cost of being repetitive, of all the statesmen that ever graced this world, and nobody was closer to perfection than Jesus. He was perfect in the true sense of the word. While we may be exposed to great leaders and different styles of leadership, none can be compared to the example of Jesus. Famous leaders cannot be discussed without any sense of pride, glory or even controversy, attached to their names. Jesus showed a style of leadership that surprised, and still does, the world today. His view and approach to leadership is contrary to what is practiced today, even in church organizations.

---

[126] Ford Leeighton – Transforming Leadership – Inter Varsity Press - 1991

In many Christian organizations today, leaders have to be acknowledged and honoured and in some cases placed on pedestals. If not, it is seen as being disrespectful. I personally have no problem with this. My concern is that, in some cases, this takes precedence. Jesus taught us a style of leadership that is juxtaposed to what the world believes in. He maintained strength is not a rule from authority but from a position of humility. The measurement of greatness was determined from a position of servant-hood. The greatest leader was, in actual fact, the greatest servant. His example is a dramatic shift of focus from preoccupation with tensions, domestic interests and agendas.

The book of Mark 10:42-44 reads:

"You know that those who are recognized as rulers of the Gentiles lord it over them. But it is not so among you, but whoever wishes to become great among you shall be your servant; and whoever wishes to be first among you shall be slave to all."

Leading from a position of authority and power is a norm of the world. Jesus said –"not so among you."

This is a radical approach that is contrary to secular belief systems, including our churches. Some aspire to leadership out of sense of adventure, some out for the satisfaction of being recognized and followed. There are some who make a genuine sacrifice out of a sense of service.

Servant-hood was the Savior's measure of determining greatness. The world system leads through manipulation, personal charisma, or subtle intimidation. This system has replicated itself in churches throughout the world. Jesus bypassed the Roman government and overlooked the local magistrates. It was the Scribes and Pharisees he took on directly. Hence, the religious system of the day was what he, not only had to contend with, but also had to deal with. The power leadership mentality of the Scribes and Pharisees has crept into the church today. This is contrary to the servant leadership displayed by Jesus.

The leadership Jesus taught us was an approach in which leaders exist in order to serve. This was contrary to the leadership experienced by the Israelites under Roman occupation, one of domination and subjugation. We don't gravitate to this type of leadership, but it happens when we give up our own interests to genuinely lookout for the wellbeing of those we are called to serve. We are responsible for those that have entrusted themselves in our care. Every one of these people has an intrinsic worth, irrespective of their social status or whatever measurement we use to classify people.

Servant leadership was not a style Jesus adopted but a reality he expressed. Humility was the yardstick of measurement. This was evidenced by people appropriating every facet of what He taught.

Philip Greenslade states:

"in a radical fashion, Jesus, by example and word, establishes servanthood as the way in which his men are to lead others. He expressly repudiates every secular model of leadership in favor of servanthood."[127]

He continuously reminded his disciples that leadership was about sacrifice and service. He continually abrogated the egotistical attitude of the disciples. This was very evident in the book of Mark 10:35-45.

Let us look at examples of the view of Jesus and the Apostles on servant leadership:

- "And do not be called leaders; for One is your Leader, that is, Christ." (Matthew 23:10)
- "But the greatest among you shall be your servant." (Matthew 23:11)
- "And whoever exalts himself shall be humbled; and whoever humbles himself shall be exalted."(Matthew 23:12)

---

[127] Greenslade Philip – Leadership, Greatness and Servanthood – Minneapolis - 1984

- Not that we lord it over your faith, but are workers with you for your joy; for in your faith you are standing firm. (2 Corinthians 1:24)

- For we do not preach ourselves but Christ Jesus as Lord, and ourselves as your bond servants for Jesus' sake. (2 Corinthians 4:5)

- Nor yet lording it over those allotted to your charge, but proving to be examples to the flock. (1 Peter 5:3).

The leadership styles of the apostles reflected the humility and service of their Lord. Peter referred to himself as a common "fellow-elder" (1 Peter 5:1). He never took the title or claimed to be the Chief Apostle.[128]

John referred to the Gentile believers as "little children" and "beloved". John proclaimed that the love for one another was the litmus test of knowing God.

Peter, Paul, John, and James continuously entrusted themselves and those under their care to the Holy Spirit.[129]

Standardization leadership

Standardization stifles freedom and de-motivates people. Highly gifted people often avoid standardized ministries because of pressure to conform. This type is often seen in certain denominational sectors.

Servant leadership allows for freedom to various methods, styles and forms. Jesus' evangelistic methods were seldom repeated. He told Nicodemus he must be born again. For the Samaritan woman, he asked for a drink of water, before dialoguing with her. To the crippled and disabled man he said, "Do you wish to get well?" (John 5:6).

---

[128] Rinehart Stacy – Upside down – NavPress – Colorado – 1998
[129] Ibid

Note that Jesus did not use standardized methods. He fitted His approach to individual needs and personalities.[130]

Jesus used a "curved ball approach." This is very evident in the parables.

Conformity leadership

Conformity treats all believers alike and expects them to act alike. Unique gifts are seldom valued or recognized. This retards both the growth of leadership and the local church. Conformity also undermines initiative and creativity. Generally, when people are pressured to conform, resistance is unavoidable. Hence, they often adopt attitudes that are contra to their personality. They are pressured into roles that are not a true representation of their gifts and talents. It is similar to being put in an incorrect mold.

Some churches have a tendency to exert pressure on people to conform on account of their traditions, denominational practices and methods. This creates barriers in accomplishing true purpose of the church in today's environment. We will fail to maintain and sustain the attention of the younger generation. This will only allow for linear thinking – logical sequence of steps with calculated moves looking for approval and validation. Inevitably, this will result in a church that will eventually become fossilized and ultimately dead.

We generally have become a generation of nonconformists because we refuse to be bound by certain precedents. While we acknowledge precedents, we are also careful that non conformism does not lead to rebellion. Is spite of this, we are patriotic, in the true sense of the Word.

Now is the time for an imaginative, creative vision orientated culture. It's time for lateral thinking, free rangers, future builders and trail blazers, who will take leaps with the view of bringing imagination into reality. While certain rules of the house have to be adhered to,

---

[130] Rinehart Stacy – Upside down – NavPress – Colorado – 1998

the general freedom of worship must be expressed with spiritual vigour and vitality. This becomes a preferred destination of empowerment.

Empowerment leadership

Servant leaders equip and develop people in ways that empower them to live according to their gifting and calling. Freedom in the Spirit is encouraged as their contributions to the body may be unique. The unity of faith propagated by Jesus allows for diversity without division and controlled conformity. There has to be a level of freedom in worship which, obviously must conform to order.

The twelve disciples that Jesus chose were diverse. They were hyper-conservative, zealously propagating nationalism. Others were considered traitors to their own country, collecting taxes for the occupying Romans. The twelve however, followed Jesus because of His compelling character.[131]

Scripture Versus Pragmatism

Pragmatism is a rejection of the idea that the function of thought is to describe, represent, or mirror reality. Instead, pragmatists develop their philosophy around the idea that the function of thought is as an instrument or tool for prediction, action, and problem solving. Pragmatists contend that most philosophical topics—such as the nature of knowledge, language, concepts, meaning, belief, and science—are all best viewed in terms of their practical uses and successes rather than in terms of representative accuracy.

Pragmatism produces ministry technicians who rely on the natural processes for empowerment. As a result of this, we embrace business models.

Business models are fashioned after management principles that are often, diametrically opposed to servant leadership espoused by Jesus.

---

[131] Ibid

Most business models are based on productivity and profitability. Servant leadership is based on relationship and people.

When the bible is allowed to speak, fresh approaches emerge and scripture becomes authoritative. The servant leader directs people to scriptures.[132]

Scripture forms the ultimate basis of our operating standards, value system and codes of conduct. In the final analysis, our true value is not only measured but determined according to scripture.

Transformation Process

Power and servant leadership is opposite of each other and has contrasting values often with different results. In spite of this, none of us live totally in either camp. Sometimes, even if we refuse to acknowledge or admit, we are always tempted to rely on some subtle form of power or manipulation to advance our own agendas. Our fallen human nature leaves room for us to do this. There is no excuse, as God has given us the perfect example of leadership to embrace. He will hold us accountable.

Servant leadership is not a form of initial internship, which gravitates to the ultimate. It is a lifelong, ongoing commitment and lasts as long as God has given us charge over his flock. Jesus' graduation was death. He was the only One to receive the ultimate.

His display of leadership, while on the face of the earth, has embedded and engraved qualities that cannot be removed from both leadership and personality traits, that must be embraced

Servant style leadership is the ultimate expression of leadership. To express means to show by means of doing. So servant leadership is not only what a leader practices, but embodies the sum total of who he is. This is easily detectable. Often times, people put on a façade as an expression of servant-hood. Eventually true character is revealed.

---

[132] Ibid

Similar to most things in life, anything that is not genuine will soon express its true form. A genuine servant attitude is primarily an expression of a changed heart. The old nature has been replaced by a new attitude. The changing of nature is only achieved through one channel.

11 Corinthians 5:17 reads:

"Therefore, if anyone is in Christ, he is a new creation; the old has gone, the new has come."

This process of change by transformation must take place. Once this happens, the true character of a servant attitude is displayed as a form of lifestyle.

In Charge Attitude

In our current day situation, we are accustomed to asking "who is in charge?" Members of the early church never asked this question because their teachings were centered on serving one another. We need to understand the resurrection of Christ was not long gone and that His physical influence was prevalent. In other words His presence was not only felt in their spirit but His physical appearance was still somewhat lingering on in their minds. Christ also left an inexplicable lasting impression that seemed as though it had been engraved on their hearts. The early leaders knew the way of serving as the only way. That way was serving one another.

As life began to progress, it became complex. This resulted in variations of leadership practices. The core concept has not changed and still remains as the ultimate in church leadership. It needs no new introduction, but just reminding us that the example set by Christ was and is servant leadership.

In Paul's technology we discussed, in detail, the model of leadership. He chose two men, Timothy and Epaphroditus. He did not choose them for their splendid oration or managerial skills, but for their selflessness. Timothy was known for his genuine interest in people. This is the first and by far the most important trait for anyone who considers taking a position of leadership, not wealth accumulation. This is the core and foundational requirement. No one should consider or be considered for leadership, if there were any doubts regarding this core value.

Philippians 2:19-20 reads:

"I hope in the Lord Jesus to send Timothy to you soon, so that I may be cheered when I receive news about you. I have no one else like him, who takes a genuine interest in your welfare."

Philippians 2:25-30 reads:

"But I think it is necessary to send back to you Epaphroditus, my brother, fellow worker and fellow soldier, who is also your messenger, whom you sent to take care of my needs.

For he longs for all of you and is distressed because you heard he was ill.

Indeed he was ill, and almost died. But God had mercy on him, and not him only but also on me, to spare me sorrow upon sorrow.

Therefore I am all the more eager to send him, so that when you see him again you may be glad and I may have less anxiety.

Welcome him in the Lord with great joy, and honor men like him.

Because he almost died for the work of Christ, risking his life to make up for the help you could not give me."

Unfortunately, in today's world, this does not appear to be the case. There are several different reasons why people consider leadership. The most prevalent reasons are authority which gives rise to power, hence, power leadership and the other being financial gains resulting in wealth accumulation. Financial gains and wealth accumulation should be a result of expressed blessings, not plundering of resources.

Power leadership has been discussed in a previous chapter. When financial gains become the reason, then focus is placed on productivity and increase. When more emphasis is placed on quantity rather than quality then leaders become income based as opposed to outcome based.

Money is an essential requirement to do anything, including doing God's work. I am not referring to this necessity but to those who express interest because of personal financial gain due to misplaced priorities.

Howard Snyder states:

The church is a theocracy, not a democracy. But it is not hierarchical theocracy tracing from God down a ladder to the lay peasant. Rather it is a family in which God rules supremely, but kindly and lovingly in a way that builds and affirms each member and makes hierarchy superfluous.[133]

Paul's criteria for leadership are relationship not positional. This boils down to serving one another. The church is not a chain of command but a network of love. This portrayal of love, once again, is centered on servant-hood.

Under the new covenant, the basis for spiritual authority is evidence of the Holy Spirit's work within a humble servant. Moses was the most humble man on the face of the earth, yet he was the most powerful man for God's power worked through humility. A leader cannot demand what he has not earned. Earned authority in God's economy is based on humility. In his letters to Timothy, Paul did not instruct Timothy to throw his authority into the faces of troublemaking church members. Rather he exhorted: "in speech, conduct, love, faith and purity show yourself an example of those who believe" (1 Timothy 4:12). Godliness rather than assumed authority was the basis for Timothy's claim to spiritual leadership.[134]

As stated earlier, a leader's estimate of humanity is revealed by the way he leads and structures his ministry. If he has a low estimate of

---

[133] Snyder A Howard –Liberating the church – Downers Grove – 1983

[134] Rinehart Stacy – Upside down – NavPress – Colorado – 1998

humanity, he leads with an iron fist and structures the ministry for tight control. If he views people as sheep, he structures the ministry for enhancement and empowerment of the flock.

Structure and organization are tools to carry out the functions of equipping the saints and winning the lost world for Christ. Servant based leadership and structures that carry ministries must have a focal point. This focal point is serving as Jesus did. Therefore, structure is used as the means to achieve the end.

Our challenge as leaders then is to create an environment that enables people to live out God's purpose in their lives. We should not let structures and organizations degenerate into forms devoid of their original functions. When this happens, our ministries become entrenched, unchallengeable, and unchangeable.[135]

Ministry of Jesus

During the time of Jesus, the entire political scene was totally controlled by the Romans. The Jews had settled into life as a conquered people living in an occupied land. The Hebrew nation was not really at home in spite of being in their country because of the Roman rule. This was the time of political stability through Roman detachments. The Roman leaders were not concerned with the welfare of the common man. Any set of beliefs, or number of deities were acceptable. They were not bothered about how the common man lived, believed in or propagated. However, any form of revolution or teachings thereof, were literally crushed with extreme force. Just as long as the people obeyed, paid their taxes and subjected themselves to Roman rule, there were no problems or concerns for the Roman leadership.

For the first time since Malachi, after several hundred years of silence, God spoke directly to the people of Israel. He spoke through Jesus

---

[135] Rinehart Stacy – Upside down – NavPress – Colorado – 1998

His Son, validating who they were. Jesus further summed up His mission in this way:

Matthew 20:28 reads:

"Just as the Son of Man did not come to be served; but to serve, and to give his life as a ransom for many."

Throughout Jesus' ministry this declaration was never contradicted unlike the lives of the religious leaders of the day. Jesus' priority was the preparation of the nation for an eternal kingdom. He was building a holy community. He dealt with the issues at hand, healing, delivering and teaching a new value system, redefining conduct and behavior for worship. This was in contrast to the teachings of the religious systems of the day. This caused a stir with the religious leaders, thus, profoundly threatening the Sanhedrin. Jesus publicly exposed the bankruptcy of the legalism that had come to define Judaism, condemning the leaders who imposed it on the people.[136]

The King James Version of the bible records the word – "leader"- only six times. Moses when addressed by God was referred as "Moses, my servant – not Moses my leader. This is what Jesus taught.

Jesus was a revolutionary, not in a guerrilla warfare sense, but with His teaching on leadership.[137]

The term servant speaks of low prestige, low honor. Most people are not attracted to such a low value role. When Jesus used this term, it was synonymous for greatness. This was a revolutionary idea.[138] Christ taught that the kingdom of God was a community where each member served one another. Paul wrote in the same vein: "serve one another in love" (Galatians 5:13).

---

[136] Refer to Matthew 23 – Mark 12:38-40 – Luke 20:45-47
[137] Sanders J Oswald – Spiritual Leadership – Moody Press- Chicago-1967
[138] Ibid

Another sharp contrast between our common ideas of leadership is found in the book of Mark 10:42-43. Jesus teaching was such a revolutionary idea that James and John used their mother in a scheme to secure top positions in the coming kingdom. These two disciples took the promise of Jesus very seriously about sitting on glorious thrones and judging the tribes of Israel (Matthew 19:28), but they misunderstood how to get there. Despite their friendship, Jesus did not give an inch to their campaign for office. His reply was "you do not know what you are asking" (Matthew 20:22). James and John wanted the glory without the cup of suffering and shame. They wanted the crown, not the cross.[139]

Jesus used this occasion to teach two principles:[140]

The Sovereignty of Spiritual Leadership: "To sit at my right or left is not for me to grant. These places belong to those for whom they have been prepared." (Mark 10:40)

God assigns places of spiritual ministry and leadership in His sovereign will. The Good News version translates verse 40 as "It is God who will give these places to those for whom He has prepared them."

The Suffering of Spiritual Leadership: "Can you drink the cup I drink and be baptized with the baptism I am baptized with?" (Mark 10:38). To this question the disciples replied that they would be able. Jesus already knew what lay ahead. They would eventually drink of the cup of suffering and therefore know the baptism. James would be executed, Peter would be crucified, and John would spend his last days in isolated confinement.

Only once in all the recorded words of Jesus did our Lord announce that He would provide an "example" for the disciples, and then he washed their feet. (John 13:15).

---

[139] Sanders J Oswald – Spiritual Leadership – Moody Press- Chicago-1967
[140] Ibid

With Jesus as the supreme example to follow, servant-hood became the rule of His body. There was no place for an authoritarian stance among the leaders, for all were under the lordship of Christ. Difference of gifts and styles were complimentary not competitive. What made this possible is their love for one another.

Romans 12:10 reads:

"Be devoted to one another in brotherly love. Honor one another above yourselves."

Those who lead first of all were servants, a quality nowhere more essential that in relationships with fellow leaders.

Example gives credibility to leadership. People are far more impressed by what they see than what they hear. Paul reminded the elders of Ephesus how he had kept back nothing that was for their good and had shown them all things. Writing to the church of Philippi, he said: "The things which ye both learned and received and heard and saw in me, these things do". (Phil 4:9) He did not invite people to follow a theory but a person. That person was Jesus Christ, the only Lord and Savior.

Jesus' teaching on servant-hood and suffering was not intended merely to inspire good behaviour. Jesus wanted to impart a spirit of servant-hood, the sense of personal commitment and identity that He expressed when He said, "I am among you as He who serves" (Luke 22:27).

In Isaiah 42, we read about the attributes and inner motives that the coming Messiah would demonstrate as the ideal servant of the Lord. Where Israel failed to live up to this ideal, the Messiah would succeed. And the principles of His life would be a pattern for ours.

Oswald J Sanders in his book *Spiritual Leadership* analyses Isaiah 42 as follows:[141]

---

[141] Sanders J Oswald – Spiritual Leadership – Moody Press- Chicago-1967

Dependence - "Here is my servant, whom I uphold" (Isaiah 42:1). This verse speaks of the coming Messiah. Jesus fulfilled the prophecy by emptying himself of divine prerogative. That is "He made himself nothing" (Phil 2:7). He surrendered the privileges of His God-nature and became dependent on His heavenly Father. He fully identified Himself with our humanity.

Approval - "My chosen one in whom I delight" (Isaiah 42:1). God took great delight in His servant Jesus. And that delight was reciprocal. In another Old Testament reference to the coming Messiah, the Son testifies, I delight to do Thy will, O my God. (Psalms 40:8)

Modesty - "He will not shout or cry out, or raise his voice in the streets" (Isaiah 42:2). Neither strident nor flamboyant, God's servant conducts a ministry that appears almost self-effacing. This is in contrast to what we see today, both in and out of church – a lot of this has already been explained.

Jesus was tempted on this very point. (Matthew 4:5). So quiet and unobtrusive is the great Servant's work that many today doubt His very existence. Jesus exemplifies the description of God later in Isaiah: "Truly you are a God who hides himself" (Isaiah 45:15).

Empathy - "A bruised reed he will not break, and a smoldering wick he will not snuff out" (Isaiah 42:3). The Lord's servant is sympathetic with a weak merciful understanding towards those who err. The ideal servant does not run over the weak and failing. He mends bruises and fans the weak spirit into a flame. How dimly Peter's own wick burned out in the judgment hall, but what a blaze on the day of Pentecost. God's ideal servant made that man's life a brilliant flame.

Optimism – "He will not falter or be discouraged till he establishes justice on earth" (Isaiah 42:4). Pessimism and leadership are at opposite ends of life's attitudes. Hope and optimism are essential qualities for the servant of God who battles with the powers of darkness over the souls of men and women. God's ideal Servant is optimistic until every part of God's work is done.

Anointing - "I will put my spirit on Him" (Isaiah 42:1). None of these leadership qualities – dependence, approval, modesty, empathy, or optimism – are sufficient for the task. Without the touch of the supernatural, these qualities are dry as dust. And so the Holy Spirit comes to rest upon and dwell in the ideal Servant. "You know… How God anointed Jesus of Nazareth with the Holy Spirit and power, and how he went around doing good" (Acts 10:37-38). Jesus' ministry began when the Spirit descended at His baptism and then began to impact the world.

Gene Wilkes in his book *Jesus on Leadership* summarizes seven principles to lead as Jesus led.[142]

1. Jesus humbled himself and allowed God to exalt him.
2. Jesus followed his Father's will rather than sought a position.
3. Jesus defined greatness as being a servant and being first as becoming a slave.
4. Jesus risked serving others because he trusted that he was God's Son.
5. Jesus left his place at the head of the table to serve the needs of others
6. Jesus shared responsibility and authority with those he called to lead.
7. Jesus built a team to carry out a worldwide vision.

Summary of Jesus' Leadership Practices:[143]

1. Jesus publicly confronted the power orientated, legalistic system and its leaders.

---

[142] Gene C Wilkes – Jesus on Leadership-Tyndale Publishers-Illinois-1998

[143] Rinehart Stacy – Upside down – NavPress – Colorado – 1998

2. His leadership style was that of a servant, even though he truly had all the power and authority of heaven.

3. He instructed His followers in unity, love and servant-hood, teaching the importance of community.

4. He did not speak of an organization, institution, or any specific structure through which the apostles were to facilitate the spread of the gospel.

5. When the religious establishment sought His death, He submitted.

Summary of the Apostles Leadership Practices:[144]

1. The Trinity was the real and practical leader of the early church.

2. The Apostles gave themselves to building up God's people rather than to organizations or hierarchies of leadership.

3. Women exercised their spiritual gifts in ministry.

4. The leadership style of the apostles flowed from a desire to serve rather than to dominate. Their demeanour exuded humility, not pride or arrogance.

5. They did not set up organizational structures to combat ever present doctrinal or leadership problems.

6. They taught that the indwelling Holy Spirit's ministry of leading and truth giving would overcome the attacks from within and without.

Summary of the Church Father's Leadership Practices:[145]

---

[144] Ibid

[145] Rinehart Stacy – Upside down – NavPress – Colorado – 1998

1. They transferred leadership from Christ the Head to human leaders and administrative structures.

2. They set up structures and infrastructures similar to Jewish and pagan religions.

3. Ignatius taught that the bishop represented God. He thus set up a hierarchy of bishops and priests.

4. Early leaders separated the church into competing organizations.

The Importance of the Kingdom for Leaders:[146]

1. The King has absolute authority. All citizens of His Kingdom are equal under his reign.

2. A church or organization is not synonymous with the kingdom of God

3. Building our own personal kingdom means hindering the progress of God's kingdom.

4. Building ministries that focus on human leaders is contrary to kingdom values.

5. Effective kingdom leadership is measured by character and relationship. It is empowered by the Holy Spirit, not ones position or personality.

6. Organizational structures should help extend kingdom citizenship to others while demonstrating kingdom values.

7. Spiritual leaders are to point people to God's kingdom, not their own kingdom.

---

[146] Ibid

The following is a list of characteristics that contrast power leadership with servant leadership:[147]

Power Leaders	Servant Leaders
• Feed on the spotlight	• Share the spotlight with others
• Are the focal point of the ministry	• Make Jesus the focal point
• Don't develop other leaders	• Develop many people
• Have a high turnover as people leave the ministry	• Have a low turnover because people stay and are loyal
• Keep the focus on themselves and their agendas	• Make Christ the central focus and agenda
• Cannot share agendas	• Affirm and participate in kingdom agendas
• Feed on being in charge and having power	• Are committed to being a servant first and foremost
• Leave people feeling hurt and abused	• Are committed to reconciliation and relationships
• Refer to their title frequently	• May have a title but seldom refer to it
• Are masters of manipulation and/or abuse those who get in their way	• Respect people for their freedom to think, act and respond.
• Use power images, offices, and perks to reveal their place	• Abhor the thought of using power images.
• Pull rank to get their way	• Never abuse people to get their way only because of their position

[147] Rinehart Stacy – Upside down – NavPress – Colorado – 1998

• Recruit many followers from their work	• Develop many followers for the Lord

Leadership begins with a mission. Without mission there is no need or motivation to lead.

Biblical servant leadership never begins with individuals wishes. Instead it finds its motivation from God's commissioning a person to carry out a divine plan.

Cyril Barber in his book, Effective Leadership quotes Sir Arthur Bryant in an article published in the *Illustrated London News*, "No one is fit to lead his followers unless he holds their care and well-being to be his prime responsibility, his duty .... his privilege."[148]

Here are some familiar examples:[149]

1. Joseph became a leader after God placed a vision in his heart to preserve his covenant people.

2. Moses became a servant leader of God when he followed God's call on his life to go to Pharaoh and deliver the message: "The Lord says, let my people go."

3. Gideon would never have been a leader if he had not followed God's mission to deliver tribes of Israel from the Midianites.

4. David became king when God, through Samuel, anointed him king. He humbly followed God's plan to assume the throne of Israel. He did not seek it.

5. Isaiah became prophet - a leader when God called him to take a message of hope and judgment to the people of Israel.

---

[148] Barber Cyril – Effective Leadership – Cox & Wyman – Berkshire - 2004
[149] Gene C Wilkes – Jesus on Leadership-Tyndale Publishers-Illinois-1998

6. Nehemiah became a remarkable leader when God commissioned him to rebuild the wall around Jerusalem.

7. Esther became a leader when God, through Mordecai, called her to stand before the king to protect the remnant of God's people.

8. Peter became a leader in the early church after Jesus commissioned him and the other disciples to make disciples of all people.

9. The apostle Paul led from a clear mission to extend the boundaries of God's grace to those outside the Jewish faith.

Jesus exhibited paradoxical styles of leadership. He adapted his style according to those he addressed and the context of the situation. His character never changed. He remained committed to the Father's call on his life. Out of that call and character, he adopted a style of leadership to meet the moment. Jesus also used paradox in his teachings. He taught:[150]

"Whoever finds his life will lose it, and whoever loses his life for my sake will find it"

Matthew 10:39

"So the last will be first, and the first will be last"

Matthew 20:16

"The kingdom of heaven is like a mustard seed"

Matthew 13:31

"Whoever humbles himself will be exalted"

Matthew 23:12

---

[150] Gene C Wilkes – Jesus on Leadership-Tyndale Publishers-Illinois-1998

1. He was gentle as a lamb yet courageous as a lion.
2. He was yielding yet aggressive when cornered by injustice.
3. He was gregarious but spent much time alone.
4. He was meek yet in control at all times.
5. He never had a formal education, yet he taught with great authority.
6. He was a conformist yet an iconoclast
7. He was a friend to the outcast yet dined with insiders.

Jesus defined greatness and leadership with paradox. He painted greatness as the work of a servant and defined leadership as the place of a slave.[151]

Servant leaders multiply their leadership by empowering others to lead.

Mark 6:7 provides the elements for this principle:[152]

"Calling the Twelve."

Jesus called the disciples to carry out this mission to reach the lost and establish his kingdom on earth. Servant leadership begins with a call to be servant to the mission of God.

"To Him"

This phase describes Jesus' role as the leader. Leaders invite others to join them on mission.

"He Sent Them out Two by Two"

This tells us that Jesus was willing to multiply his leadership in others. Teams of at least two followers were part of his strategy for this.

---

[151] Ibid

[152] Gene C Wilkes – Jesus on Leadership-Tyndale Publishers-Illinois-1998

Jesus demonstrated that implementing a mission is not an individual effort. Teams are the best vehicle by which to do God's work.

"(He) Gave Them Authority Over Evil Spirits."

Jesus empowered those he called. We will see later how Jesus modeled empowerment for his followers.

Leadership of a team is the highest expression of servant leadership. This is true because team leadership embodies each of the principles of servant leadership.[153]

1. You must humble yourself in order to build a team. Humility allows you to see the need for others. Pride insists on working alone.

2. You cannot seek a position and have the team succeed. Following Jesus keeps you on the mission and out of competition with others.

3. You must be willing to give up your personal right to be served and find greatness in service to the mission and the other team members.

4. You must trust that God is in control of your life in order to risk service to those on the team.

5. You must take up the towel of service to meet the needs of the group.

6. You must share both responsibility and authority with team members in order to meet the greater need of the team's goal

7. You must multiply your leadership by empowering other members of the team to lead.

---

[153] Gene C Wilkes – Jesus on Leadership-Tyndale Publishers-Illinois-1998

8. Team ministry is how servant leaders do the work of mission. In our servant leadership model we see that team is how the leader best serves those he has recruited.

Hudson Taylor, founder of the China Inland Mission, in his letter dated 1879 to the secretary of the mission said:[154]

The all-important thing to do is to:

1. Improve the character of the work
2. Deepen the piety, devotion and success of the workers
3. Remove stones of stumbling, if possible
4. Oil the wheels where they stick
5. Amend whatever is defective
6. Supplement, as far as may be, what is lacking.

Such simple advice reveals insight into a leader's responsibility. An analysis highlights six important areas to care for.

Administration – to improve the character of the work. The leader must discover which departments are functioning below standards and remedy the defect. This may involve developing new job descriptions, or establishing new reporting procedures and other lines of communications.

Spiritual tone – to deepen the piety, devotion, and success of the worker. The tone of the church or mission will be a reflection of its leaders. Water rises to the level of its source. The spiritual health of the leadership group should be a top concern among higher echelon leadership. Job satisfaction is also important. If leaders can show their colleagues methods to improve success, their sense of fulfilment will be reflected in an improvement in the quality of their work.

---

[154] Sanders J Oswald – Spiritual Leadership – Moody Press- Chicago-1967

Group morale – to remove stones of stumbling. Friction among a team should be minimized. When problems are neglected, morale drops and performance decreases. If the problem has a remedy, it should be put into place at once. If the problem is a person, the delinquent should be dealt with as soon as the facts are clear. The problem or person should be treated with consideration and love, but the work of God cannot be sacrificed for the sake of keeping peace.

Personal relationships – to oil the wheels when they stick. Warm relationships among team members are vital. Some workers prefer to administer; others want to love people. Only the latter are leaders. In handling people, the oil can is much more effective than the acid bottle.

Problem solving – to amend what is defective. One of the chief duties of leaders is to solve tough problems within the organization. Creating problems is easy; solving them is difficult. The leader must face the problem realistically, and follow through until the solution is reached.

Creative planning – to supplement what is lacking. Criticizing plans is easier than creating them. The leader must see the goal clearly, plan imaginatively, and employ tactics that lead to success. In this department there is always a short supply of people ready and qualified to perform.

One more way to improve leadership potential: resist the idea of "leadership from the rear." True leadership is always from the top down, never from the bottom up. It was the leadership from the rear that led Israel back into the wilderness.

Many churches and organization are in a stalemate because leaders have submitted to the kind of blackmail from the rear. No dissident or reactionary element should be allowed to determine group policy against the consensus of the spiritual leaders.[155]

---

[155] Sanders J Oswald – Spiritual Leadership – Moody Press- Chicago-1967

Leading from a posture of humility

Thus far we have encountered two contrasting concepts or styles of leadership – power leadership and servant leadership- which have been, and still are, active in every facet of ministry and ministries. It has now also become clear as to what spiritual leadership is and what it is not. Scriptures have clearly defined both concepts and styles. It has been evidenced several times that unless we follow the pattern of Jesus example, we will conform to structures that have been built that create power houses. These power structures determine patterns for which we will govern or rule instead of leading according to God's order and example.

Our basis of leadership must be correct:

Not power based

Not power controlled

Not power peopled

Not power structured

The Apostle Paul outlines an excellent example in 1 Corinthians 1: 29 and 2:6:

"Brothers, think of what you were when you were called. Not many of you were wise by human standards; not many were influential; not many were of noble birth. But God chose the foolish things of the world to shame the wise; God chose the weak things of the world to shame the strong. He chose the lowly things of this world and the despised things – and the things that are not – to nullify the things that are, so that no one may boast before him.

It is because of him that you are in Christ Jesus, who has become for us wisdom from God – that is, our righteousness, holiness and redemption. Therefore, as it is written: "Let him who boasts boast in the Lord."

When I came to you, brothers, I did not come with eloquence or superior wisdom as I proclaimed to you the testimony about God. For I resolved to know nothing while I was with you except Jesus Christ and Him crucified. I came to you in weakness and fear, and with much trembling. My message and my preaching were not with wise and persuasive words, but with a demonstration of the Spirit's power, so that your faith might not rest on men's wisdom, but on God's power. We do, however, speak a message of wisdom among the mature, but not the wisdom of this age or of the rulers of this age, who are coming to nothing.

The majority of leaders began with a genuine heart to serve. However, for some reason, our human nature seems to take control in our quest for power.

If you are greatly gifted, you may be able to do marvelous things that would cause the public to be swept up in your skills and in your abilities. In the process of your growing, you will find great temptation to make a name for yourself, to make a big splash, to gain attention, to get glory, to strut around, to increase your fees, to demand your rights, and expect kid-glove treatment."[156]

The ways of the Christian Leader is not the way of upward mobility in which our world has invested so much, but the way of downward mobility ending on the cross.[157]

There is a dire need for leadership in today's world to move away from the power model and mentality and embrace the paradox of servant leadership. We need leaders that will serve people – leaders who will put the needs of others and the ministry above their own. This is the pen-ultimate sacrifice. We need to embrace the methodology of Jesus and also pay careful consideration to the technologies displayed by the various Apostles.

---

[156] Charles Swindol – Living above the Lever of Mediocrity – Waco Texas - 1987

[157] Nouwen Henri – Reflections on Christian Leadership – New York - 1989

1 Peter 5:2-4 reads:

"Shepherd the flock of God which is among you, serving as overseers, not by compulsion but willingly, not for dishonest gain but eagerly; nor as being lords over those entrusted to you, but being examples to the flock; and when the Chief Shepherd appears; you will receive the crown of glory that does not fade away."

In the book of John, Chapter 15, Jesus makes it very clear that there is a much more serious consideration, much more than success and achievement. Abiding in Him will result in bearing fruit. This is the true test of a genuineness of a servant. Servant-hood is about fruitfulness and reproduction. It flows from a leader who is in tune with sincerity of heart, faithful in service and authentic in service.

Conclusion

The biblical mandate on the concept of leadership, has not only been mapped out, but given as a living example depicted by our Lord Jesus Christ himself. His example of Servant Leadership has been a formula that has worked for centuries and is still very relevant today. We have distorted this view and have concluded our own interpretation, giving rise to the subject of leadership being complex. In essence, it's not!

Leadership is about scars not stars! When Jesus identified himself to his disciples after this death and resurrection, his scars were a means of identification (John 20:20, 26-29).

At the conclusion of John's long life, he reminded all "This is how we know what love is: Jesus Christ laid down his life of us. And we ought to lay down our lives for our brothers" 1 John 3.16.

In Hebrews 11 – we are presented with the leadership hall of fame. We are reminded of a group of people whose lives are characterized by sacrificial service, torture, being flogged, jeered, chained and imprisoned, stoned, sawn in two and put to death by the sword.

The cost of leadership demands total commitment. Leith Anderson quoted by Eddie Gibbs- Leadership Next – counsel us to re-assess on a continual basis the following:

- Look at the kingdom, not just your corner.
- See beyond our circumstances to the presence of Christ with us.
- Focus on successes, not problems.
- Beware of exaggerating problems and empowering failures.
- Keep a list of blessings and successes.

- Look at reality with all of its imperfections, not just exceptions.
- Re-confirm your call rather than be swayed by complaints.[158]

While many organizations choose leaders on the basis of their personalities, academic qualifications or connections, the important criteria must not be overlooked. Knowledge must be one of the prerequisites of competency. There has to be a continuous evaluation of our competency levels, strength and weaknesses, and always striving towards self-improvement. However, being conversant with all of the statistics, details, figures and technical matters does not necessarily define the traits of leadership. Leadership ultimately, involves people and getting people involved.

There is a dire need for the church to get back to basics by reviewing leadership hierarchies and structures. Let this be a working document that views a practical approach, differentiating leadership styles and patterns for adoption and discarding.

Until we get to the point of origin, we will continue to function across the grain resulting in setting up and creating basis for power structures. Scripture demands that we follow the example of our Lord Jesus and develop principles based on His model. When this happens, there will be a noted 180 degree turnabout. A different perception will be born that will redefine your code of conduct and value systems. Singular, e.g. I or me, becomes us and we. A concept based on biblical principles will prevail and the challenges of leadership will become a workable and viable concept within our organizations.

Herein, lies a huge opportunity, if we embrace the fundamentals basics of leadership. Our effort, will in turn, empower others. We become transformational leaders. We become embracers and includers. Others abilities and enthusiasm are not a threat to us. We are not creators of alliances but builders of Nations. We are unified in diversity with patience and fortitude. In spite of limited resources

---

[158] Gibbs Eddie-Leadership Next- Intervarsity Press – UK -2005

and unanticipated setbacks, we still continue with the dynamism of the Great Commission. We are conscious of economic disparity and generational differences, yet strive on unity and inclusion. We identify synergies and thrive on positive outcomes. We become kingdom seekers and not empire builders. We reproduce ourselves in others through empowering them. Success without a successor is failure. This will reduce stress levels, burnout, and create a positive workforce. We are never complete, but always a work in progress.

Attitudes reflect character. We can encourage and empower or discourage and marginalize. A good leader must have ethos, pathos and logos. Ethos is his moral character, the source of his ability to persuade. Pathos is his ability to touch feelings, to engage people on an emotional level. Logos is the ability to solidify reasons for any action, to also engage people on an emotional level.[159]

Our ministries will become productive. There will be a revolutionary change in paradigms. During this process, old type perceptions of leadership will change. Attitudes will change. Adjustments will not only become necessary, but inevitable. We will start to progress at greatly reduced effort levels.

We will not only leave a legacy but a healthy organization. This legacy will live on in the actions of many generations to come. Jesus was the supreme example of this. Over two thousand years later – the church still exists.

As John Maxwell says "You are most valuable where you add the most value. "Let your value become the legacy that will be felt in generations to come!

---

[159] Barber Cyril – Effective Leadership –Cox and Wyman – Berkshire - 2004

Leadership Dynamics

During my research, I have discovered some gems, which I call leadership dynamics. Each of these can constitute a leadership study on its own. I have included all of these in the hope that whenever it is read, it will reflect a mirror image of a true sense of leadership.

Why Read

"Read to refill the wells of inspiration," was the advice of Harold Ockenga, who took a suitcase of books on his honeymoon![160]

- Spiritual leaders should read for intellectual growth. This will require books to test wits, provide fresh ideas, challenge assumptions, and probe complexities.

- The leader should read to cultivate his preaching and writing style. Nothing can equal the writing of those masters who enlarge our vocabularies, teach us to think, and instruct us in the art of incisive and compelling speech.

- The leader should read to acquire new information, to keep current with the times, to be well informed in his or her field of expertise.

- The leader should read to have fellowship with great minds. Through books we hold communion with the greatest spiritual leaders of the ages.

- A book has great power. In Curiosities of Literature, Benjamin Disraeli gives a number of instances where a person has been magnificently influenced by a solitary book.

- A leader's reading is the outward expression of his inner hungers and aspirations. The vast number of titles pouring from presses today makes discriminating choice essential.

---

[160] Ockenga Harold J – Christianity Today - 1966

Our reading should be regulated by who we are and what we intend to accomplish.[161]

Use these rules for making your reading worthwhile and profitable:[162]

- What you intend to quickly forget, spend little time reading. The habit of reading and forgetting only builds the habit of forgetting other important matters.
- Use the same discrimination in choosing books as in choosing friends.
- Read with pencil and notebook in hand. Unless your memory is unusually retentive, much gained from reading is lost in a day. Develop a system of note-taking. It will greatly help the memory.
- Have a book to record what is striking, interesting, and worthy of second thought. In that way you will build a treasure trove of material for future use.
- Verify historical, scientific, and other data.
- Pass no word until its meaning is known.
- Vary your reading to keep your mind out of a rut. Variety is as refreshing to the mind as it is to the body.
- Correlate your reading – read on relating subjects.

Rules For Life

Rules for life that carry relevance today:[163]

- Eagerly start the day's main work.

---

[161] Sanders J Oswald – Spiritual Leadership – Moody Press- Chicago-1967
[162] Sanders J Oswald – Spiritual Leadership – Moody Press- Chicago-1967
[163] Sanders J Oswald – Spiritual Leadership – Moody Press- Chicago-1967

- Do not murmur at your busyness or the shortness of time, but buy up the time all around.

- Never murmur when correspondence is brought in.

- Never exaggerate duties by seeming to suffer under the load, but treat all responsibilities as liberty and gladness.

- Never call attention to crowded work or trivial experiences.

- Before confrontation or censure, obtain from God a real love for the one at fault. Know the facts; be generous in your judgment. Otherwise, how ineffective, how unintelligible or perhaps provocative your well intentioned censure may be.

- Do not believe everything you hear; do not spread gossip.

- Do not seek praise, gratitude, respect, or regard for past service.

- Avoid complaining when your advice or opinion is not consulted, or having been consulted, set aside.

- Never allow yourself to be placed in a favorable contrast with anyone.

- Do not press conversation to your own needs and concerns.

- Seek no favors, nor sympathies; do not ask for tenderness, but receive what comes.

- Bare the blame; do not share or transfer it.

- Give thanks when credit for your own work or ideas is given to another.

Five Types of Leadership

There are five basic types of leadership and governmental structure common in the world and in the Church. The Church has embraced all but two of them in recent years.[164]

Autocracy - This form of government features one person who possesses unlimited power and authority while, in theory, answering to no one. The foolish King Rehoboam epitomized this kind of domineering ruler and government. (1 Kings 12:1-11)

Bureaucracy - The Pharisees perfectly represent the ultimate hierarchy of authority. This system of leadership is marked by a near-worship of the methodology rather than a concern for ruling wisely or according to a true standard of right and wrong.

Democracy - This is commonly called "government by the people" and the "rule of the majority." In church circles, it is called congregationalism. Although it sounds good, the "majority" can be a cruel task master and rarely places truth and right over self and self-serving "majority rule." Its only chance of working is totally dependent on the wisdom, character, and self-restraint of the "majority."

Theocracy - This term defines the government of a state by immediate divine guidance. In this system, the rule of God is administered through delegated men and women whom He places in the church to represent Him. It only works as long as the people are confident that God actually speaks to men, and secondly, that God speaks to the leaders over them. This was God's chosen governmental method for Israel until her elders formed a committee and "voted" to reject theocracy in favor of the autocracy of a king. (1 Samuel 8:4-7).

Servant Leaders - The New Testament is filled with examples of a servant leader in action. The greatest servant of all was Jesus, who

---

[164] Munien Robert – Apostles, Apostolic People and Churches – Genesis Communications –Mobile 1999

demonstrated the importance of servant-hood in leadership by washing His disciples' feet and commanding them to do the same. (Matthew 20:25-27)

The Four Faces of Leadership

Wise leaders, especially those serving in a ministry team, understand the "four faces of leadership" revealed in Ezekiel 1:10 and fulfilled in Jesus Christ. They also know how to apply each one of them in season:[165]

Face of a man - Like the Son of man, we must be able to feel the infirmities of others, understand their hurts and needs, and relate to them while sharing their burdens.

Face of a lion - In times of trouble and times of spiritual warfare, we must know when and how to roar like the Lion of Judah with the authority and awesome power of God that dwells within us.

Face of an ox - Ministry team members must know what it means to take up the yoke of Jesus and put their shoulder to the yoke. Hard work and dedication in the face of impossible odds must be engrained in our character.

Face of an eagle - When the storm clouds approach, we must be able to ascend above the winds, the lightning, and the thunder into the very rest of God. Then we must be able to hear God's voice clearly and to discern and see into the things of God with accuracy.

Leadership Tips

1. Leaders do not have to set goals, but they see that goals are set and clearly understood.

2. Leaders do not have to decide, but must ensure that the decisions are made.

---

[165] Munien Robert – Apostles, Apostolic People and Churches – Genesis Communications –Mobile 1999

3. Leaders do not have to admonish malcontents but they must make certain that trouble makers stay in line.

When members fail in their group obligations, it imposes leadership functions on others. Effective leaders know that when a leadership void develops they must fill the gap, either by providing the leadership themselves or by encouraging others to do so. Effective leaders have learned when to take the initiative. This required knowledge of participants typically functions in groups.

4. Leaders need to work to create a non-threatening climate. Effective leaders will take no constructive directions until members feel free to express themselves.

5. Convey warmth, acceptance and empathy

6. Attending to what others say. Show attentiveness to what others are saying.

7. Understand meaning and intents. Effective leaders try to reflect on the intent of the speakers as well as what they say.[166]

A Pattern for Leadership

1. God's leaders like David and Moses must handle criticism and outright antagonism by retreating to their fortress in God. They must refuse to touch God's anointed, but choose instead to throw their whole being at the grace and mercy of God who called them in the first place. Both men suffered humiliating betrayal from their family members, but each of them were openly saved and vindicated by God Himself. Moses and David felt that if they were saved, it would be by God's hand. There were times when every man's hand seemed to be against them – even though they knew that God had anointed them to lead. Their sure Fortress remains our Fortress today.

---

[166] D'Souza Anthony – Leadership – Paulines Publications – 2003

2. The leaders for any new move of God must understand that they are heirs of the past. They must honour the past moves of God and respect the vessels that he anointed and used to bring those moves to pass. We will fail if we don't recognize the fact that we are products of what God did with our fathers before us. We are, and we have, a rich inheritance, and it is all bound up and rooted in the King of Glory, the Creator, and the Lord Jesus Christ.

3. Anointed leaders in any move of God must understand and accept their responsibilities as custodians or stewards of the present. The present generation, not the generations past or the generations yet to come are responsible for serving this present generation and establishing the Church in the present truth – not for building grand monuments to their accomplishments or to those of leaders in the past. The only altars in the new covenant Church are the altars of the heart, and they are consecrated to only one leader: The Lord Jesus Christ.

4. The leaders today are also expected to be architects and designers who will give shape to the future. God holds leaders personally responsible for leaving a legacy for the generations to come. God said to Abraham, "For I know him, that he will command his children and his household after him, and they shall keep the way of the Lord, to do justice and judgment; that the Lord may bring upon Abraham that which he hath spoken of him" (Gen 18:19).[167]

Handling Criticism

How did David handle such malicious criticism from Saul, the Israelites, Michal, and his own family members for so many years?

---

[167] Munien Robert-Understanding the Seasons of God-1998

1. David cast his cares upon the Lord. Again and again in the Psalms, we see how David poured out his sorrows to the Lord and allowed His Spirit to lift him up.

2. Though King Saul sought David's life, David did not want to "get even" with his persecutor.

3. For better or worse, David had respect for Saul's season.

4. David gave honor to Saul's leadership. He did more than talk; he backed up his words with actions. Even at the worst of times, Saul was always "the King," not "that nut who is always trying to kill me."

5. David specifically called Saul "the Lord's anointed," even when Saul had backslidden into witchcraft through his rebellion, and later even consulted a "diviner" or medium for guidance.

6. Although he had the power and resources to do so, David waited upon God to give the kingdom to him. He recognized that God is the source of all true authority.

7. David behaved himself wisely.

8. In the "song of the bow" found in 2 Samuel 1, David displays genuine sorrow and grief over Saul's death.

9. Rather than gloat and make a public announcement celebrating the downfall of his mortal enemy, David did not want the opposing army to know of Saul's defeat.

10. David personally reminded the people of all the exploits Saul had done on their behalf. He honored the fallen king as the anointed of God and the fallen leader of Israel.

11. David constantly focused on the good rather than on the bad, even though he had many occasions when there seemed to be more bad than good happening to him.

12. David knew that God alone was the source of his strength and authority. If he was ever to ascend to the throne, it would be because God put him there, not man.[168]

How did Moses react to bitter criticism that came from members of his own family?

Numbers 12:1-4 reads:

"And Miriam and Aaron spake against Moses because of the Ethiopian woman whom he had married: for he had married an Ethiopian women. And they said, Hath the Lord indeed spoken only by Moses? Hath he not spoken also by us? And the Lord heard it. (Now the man Moses was very meek, above all the men which were upon the face of the earth.) And the Lord spake suddenly unto Moses, and unto Aaron, and unto Miriam, Come out ye three unto the tabernacle of the congregation. And they three came out."

1. Miriam became jealous and resentful over Moses' interracial marriage to a non-Jewish woman. This never came up before God's children left Egypt. The problem rose shortly after Moses set aside the Levites and Aaron for the priesthood and the 70 elders were set apart for leadership. Perhaps this gave Aaron and Miriam a sympathetic audience.

2. God handled the judgment and punishment but left the task of praying for mercy to Moses, who quickly asked mercy for his sister.

Another example of how Moses handled public criticism when he was confronted by a Levite priest name Korah and his friends, along with 250 princes of Israel.

Numbers 16:3-5 reads:

---

[168] Munien Robert-Understanding the Seasons of God-1998

"And they gathered themselves together against Moses and against Aaron, and said unto them, Ye take too much upon you, seeing all the congregation are holy, everyone of them, and the Lord is among them: wherefore then lift ye up yourselves above the congregation of the Lord? And when Moses heard it, he fell upon his face: And he spake unto Korah and unto all his company, saying, even tomorrow the Lord will show who are his, and who is holy; and will cause him to come near unto him: even him whom he hath chosen to come near unto him."

Moses' response was to fall on his face before God. If any defense was to be made, it would be made by God Almighty. Korah rebelled even further against the authority of Moses and Aaron when he "gathered all the congregation against them unto the door of the tabernacle of the congregation... (Numbers6:19). God's response was quick and deadly. Korah and his friends were swallowed by the earth along with their families, and the 250 princes were consumed by fire, even as they offered incense to the Lord.[169]

What Is A True Leader?

The following is taken from Dr. Myles Munroe:[170]

1. True leadership is an attitude rather than a title. It inspires rather than manipulates or controls.
2. Influence alone is not leadership. Leadership is the capacity to influence others through inspiration motivated by a passion, generated by a vision, produced by a conviction, ignited by a purpose.
3. Leadership is not pursuit but a result.
4. Leader is not a label that you give yourself. Leadership is a privilege given by the followers.

---

[169] Munien Robert-Understanding the Seasons of God-1998

[170] Munroe Myles – The Spirit of Leadership – USA - 2005

5. Leaders inspire by expressing their inner passion, which then resonates with others and causes them to join in pursuing the leader's visions.

6. The source of inspiration is passion.

7. True leadership passion is the discovery of a belief, reason, idea, conviction, or cause not just to live for, but also to die for, which focuses on benefiting mankind as a whole.

8. Passion comes from purpose.

9. True inspiration is not manipulation or brainwashing but an invitation to pursue something higher and better than one has had before, and in the process gain a sense of meaning and significance for one's life.

10. Leaders are often ordinary people who accept or are placed under extraordinary circumstances that bring forth their latent potential, producing a character that inspires confidence and trust within others.

11. The greatest leadership seems to surface during times of personal, social, economic, political, and spiritual conflict.

12. Having followers is not a prerequisite for being a leader. The demands of leadership may require that you stand alone in the face of conflict, public opinion, or crisis.

13. Inspiration is the "divine deposit destiny" in the heart of a person.

14. What you are gifted in often reveals what type of leadership you are meant to exercise and what domain you are to operate in.

15. True leaders discover keys to the nature of leadership from the examples of others, but they never try to become these other leaders. They use their own gifts and abilities to do what they are individually called to do.

16. Failing to discover or pursue your personal leadership potential will deprive your generation and succeeding generations of your unique and vital contribution to the world.[171]

The Leadership Ability

Munroe further illustrates leadership ability.[172]

1. Leadership is both aptitude and an attitude.

2. No leader can raise his or her attitude.

3. Man's greatest challenge is having his attitude correspond with the mind of the Spirit of God within him.

4. The mind of the Spirit is the presence of the Spirit of God in man's spirit, but the spirit of the mind is the attitude that accompanies that spirit.

5. Salvation is not necessarily synonymous with conversion. The word conversion in Greek means "reversion" or "a turning about." We need to revert to the original information the Manufacturer gave us.

6. It is through the Spirit of the Creator that we can mend the attitude of our minds because He is the Spirit of Truth who reminds us of the truth that the Authorized Dealer brought us.

7. You have to patiently allow the new information from the Creator to settle into your subconscious.

---

[171] Munroe Myles – The Spirit of Leadership – USA - 2005
[172] Munroe Myles – The Spirit of Leadership – USA – 2005

Bibliography

1. Abbey, R. Merril. 1967. *Communication in Pulpit and Parish,* Westminster Press, Philadelphia.
2. Barber Cyril. Effective Leadership, Cox & Wyman, Berkshire. 2004
3. Barclay, Williams. 1960. *Letters to Timothy and Titus,* Edinburgh.
4. Bob, Briner & Ray, Pritchard. 1997. *Leadership Lessons of Jesus,* Broadman & Holman.
5. Cha, John. *10 Pillars of Leadership,* Teamwork Publication.
6. Charles, Swindol. 1987. *Living above the Lever of Mediocrity,* Waco Texas.
7. D'Souza. Anthony. 1994. *Developing the Leader within You,* Singapore.
8. D'Souza Anthony, Leadership, Paulines Publications, 2003
9. Farrar, Steven. 1994. *Standing Tall,* Questar Publishers.
10. Ford Leeighton. Transforming Leadership, Inter Varsity Press. 1991
11. Foster, J. Richard. 1978. *Celebration of Discipline,* Harper and Row.
12. Gibbs Eddie. Leadership Next, Intervarsity Press, UK. 2005
13. Gardner, John. 1990. *On Leadership,* The Free Press.
14. Greenleaf, Robert. 1967. *Servant Leadership*, Paulis Press, New York.
15. Greenslade, Philip. 1984. *Leadership, Greatness and Servanthood,* Minneapolis.
16. Halsey, George. 1966. *Supervising People*
17. Hans, Seyle. 1976. *The Stress of Life*, McGraw Hill, New York.
18. Hendrikson, William. 1959. *1 and 2 Timothy and Titus,* London.

19. Hersey, P and Blanchard, K. 1977. *Organisational Behaviour*, New Jersey.
20. Horton, Scott. Michael. 1992. *Selling out of the Evangelical Church,* Moody. Chicago.
21. James, Gill. 1983. *Educating for Leadership*, Stogill.
22. Johansen, David and Van, Vonderen Jeff. 1991. *The Subtle Power of Spiritual Abuse*, Minneapolis, Bethany.
23. Jowett, J.H. *The Epistles of Peter,* Hodder & Stoughton, London.
24. Keating, Charles. 1982. *The Leadership Book,* New York.
25. Kouzes and Posner. The Leadership Challenge.
26. Lippit, L. Gordon. 1969. *Organisational Renewal,* Appleton, Century Cross, New York.
27. Marshall, Tom. 1981. *Understanding Leadership*, Clays Limited, England.
28. McGrath, Alister. 1992. *Power Religion,* Moody, Chicago.
29. Means, E. James. 1989. *Leadership in Christian Ministry,* Grand Rapids.
30. Mitchell, Costa. 1991. *Intimacy in Marriage,* Struikhof, Cape Town.
31. Munien, Robert. 1999. *Apostles, Apostolic People and Churches – Genesis Communications,* Mobile.
32. Munien, Robert. 1998. *Understanding the Seasons of God.*
33. Munroe, Myles. 1998. *Seasons of Change,* USA.
34. Munroe, Myles. 2005. *The Spirit of Leadership,* USA.
35. Nouwen, Henri. 1989. *Reflections on Christian Leadership,* New York.
36. Ockenga, Harold. J. 1966. *Christianity Today.*
37. Peters, Thomas. 1982. *In Search of Excellence*, New York
38. Peterson H Eugene – Run With The Horses – Intervarsity Press- Downers Grove – 1983

39. Peterson, Jim. 1992. *Church Without Walls,* NavPress. Colorado.
40. Powell, John. 1969. *Why I am afraid to tell you who I am?* Tabor Publishing.
41. Rees, S. Paul. *Triumphant in Trouble,* Marshall, Morgan and Scott- London
42. Rinehart, Stacy. 1998. *Upside down*, NavPress, Colorado.
43. Sanders, J. Oswald. 1967. *Spiritual Leadership,* Moody Press.
44. Shaw George Bernard –Pygmalion –quote by Anthony D'Souza – leadership – Paulines Publication 2003
45. Snyder, A. Howard. 1998. *Signs of the Spirit,* Grand Rapids.
46. Snyder, A. Howard. 1983. *Liberating the church,* Downers Grove.
47. Stanley Andy – The Next Generation Leader – Colorado - 2003
48. Strafford, John. 1987. *Effective Management*, Heinemann London.
49. Ways, Max. 1964. *The Era of Radical Change,* Fortune.
50. Wilkers, C. Gene. 1996. *Jesus Leadership Lifeway,* Press- Illinois.

www.ingramcontent.com/pod-product-compliance
Lightning Source LLC
Chambersburg PA
CBHW060523100426
42743CB00009B/1417